GU00838681

CHILDREN'S DAY

A Play

KEITH WATERHOUSE

and

WILLIS HALL

SAMUEL FRENCH

LONDON
NEW YORK   TORONTO   SYDNEY   HOLLYWOOD

FT1096

CHILDREN'S DAY

Characters:

Robin Partridge, a publisher
Emma Partridge, his wife
Peter Butler, a restaurateur
Polly Butler, his wife
Tom Sutton, Emma's solicitor
Mavis Pawson, Emma's mother's help
Sophie Lovelady, a Chelsea Girl

The action passes in the kitchen of Emma's house in Hampstead

ACT I   An afternoon in late autumn

ACT II
  Scene 1   Immediately following
  Scene 2   About an hour later

Time–the present

ACT I

The semi-basement kitchen of a large family house in Hampstead. An after-noon in late autumn

The house belongs to Emma, the estranged wife of a publisher, Robin Partridge. She lives here with her two children, Adam (five) and Charity (seven), whom we never see, and a mother's help, Mavis Pawson, a solid girl from the North. The kitchen reflects the good health of Robin's bank account, and the good taste of his wife, while owing something to the Sunday Times *colour supplement, Habitat, and the Portobello Road. There has been a certain amount of conversion, and now a narrow open staircase leads directly up from the kitchen to the door opening on to the ground-floor hall. Large french windows look out on a walled garden from which there are steps leading up to pavement level. A door leads to the larder. The kitchen table and chairs are stripped pine. The sink unit is on the invisible wall, and so what we see is a warm, pleasant picture of farmhouse life as it is lived by Hampstead families*

When the CURTAIN *rises a party is in progress upstairs—it is Adam's birthday. All the guests are between five and eight, the products of local preparatory schools. We never see them, but we are aware of their noisy presence whenever the landing door is opened*

Polly Butler, a close friend of Emma's, is alone in the kitchen. She sits in a rocking chair idly blowing up a balloon. Both the french windows and the door leading to the hall are open. From upstairs we can hear the babble of children's voices partly drowning the sound of a record player which is playing any popular childrens' L.P. record. Some guests have just arrived and Emma, who is standing at the top of the stairs, is saying good-bye to their mother through the open door. Emma is holding two children's coats under her arm

Emma Now there's no need to worry. We'll get him settled in and then we'll take his head off at tea-time. I'm sure he'll enjoy himself. And you'll collect him at six-thirty. Don't worry! 'Bye! (*Emma closes the door and immediately drops the fixed smile she had been wearing for the benefit of the parent. She rushes agitatedly downstairs*) I told her fifteen times it wasn't fancy dress and she's brought Nigel as a bloody goose. (*Without pause she rushes across to the drawer of the Welsh dresser and among the litter of string and kitchen oddments locates a meat skewer. She holds* *it up*) Skewer. Marie Louise Pollock's dropped her wristwatch down the loo.

Still carrying the coats, and the skewer, Emma rushes up the stairs again. Polly, in alarm, lets go of the balloon, which whizzes round the kitchen

Polly I thought Marie Louise had the mumps?
Emma If she has we've got an epidemic.

Emma exits, slamming the hall door behind her, and the noise of the party is cut off. Polly's husband, Peter, enters through the french windows. He is carrying a folding card table in each hand and holding a number of envelopes and a package under his arm

Polly There, you see! Marie Louise Pollock has a wristwatch and *she's* only five.
Peter I don't care if she's got a French striking clock. Matthew gets a watch when he learns to tell the time. (*He puts the tables with some collapsible wooden chairs which are stacked by the wall*) Will that be all or do the kiddiewinks want the poker chips as well? (*Holding up the envelopes and the package*) Birthday cards. I just met the postman. Pass them on to Adam, would you?
Polly You're not going?
Peter (*putting the envelopes and the package down on the table*) Of course I'm going.
Polly Peter! Emma's expecting you to lend a hand.
Peter If Adam's dear mummy wants to stroll round to the Bistro and knock up a *pâté maison* from three dozen chicken livers, I'll happily stay here and spoon out blancmange. Otherwise—(*moving to leave*)—I'll be home about midnight.
Polly Peter!
Peter The Bistro doesn't run itself.
Polly Oh, really? I often get the impression that it does.
Peter What's that supposed to mean?
Polly Only that whenever you spend the afternoon with your chicken livers you never seem to answer the phone.
Peter I don't answer the phone.
Polly Supposing I was a customer wanting a table?
Peter It might have eluded you, Polly, but cooking is an art which demands concentration.
Polly (*sweetly*) I know that you spend a lot of time with your dish of the day.

Peter reacts at this, but before he can reply, Polly, who is now looking at a child's painting on the wall, changes the subject

Polly What a super picture! I wonder which one of them painted it? Adam or Charity? Charity I should think. It's got her feeling for character.

Peter (*also looking at the painting*) Very good. What is it? A potato?

Polly It's Robin, you fool.

Peter (*looking closely*) Is it? So it is.

Polly I should think it's a reject from the *Sunday Times* Paint-Your-Daddy Competition.

Peter I'm not surprised Daddy packed his bags and left home, if that's how his offspring see him.

Polly *I'm* surprised she didn't give him horns and a tail. Walking out on Emma like that—I still can't get over it.

Peter You've been saying that twice a week for the last year. Why can't you get your vicarious pleasures out of television like anyone else?

Polly You don't understand what it's like for Emma. Left in this great barn with two kids to bring up.

Peter (*sarcastically*) I pity them! Look at it—one step up from an LCC hostel! And Robin still pays his whack for this place, you know.

Polly He barely gives her enough to exist on. Anyway, there's more to raising a family than settling the gas bill. Take Julian Syminton. He was left fatherless at the age of three and we all know what happened to him.

Peter Julian turned that way after he joined the Brigade of Guards.

Polly Heavens, a husband has to show *some* responsibility. He can't just up and off when the fancy takes him.

Peter The upping and offing in this case was by mutual consent.

Polly Was it? When a husband deserts his wife for a teenage nymphomaniac the consent is usually more mutual on one side than on the other. By the way, is it true that *she's* out on her ear now?

Peter Who?

Polly You *know* who. You-know-who.

Peter Who's you-know-who?

Polly The nymphet of Notting Hill. Has he chucked her out?

Peter I wouldn't know.

Polly You're supposed to be his friend. Of course you know.

Peter I've never bothered to ask. (*Changing the subject*) I wish Matthew would paint. He never does anything creative.

Polly Nonsense. He was painting all day yesterday.

Peter I was thinking of some more adventurous medium than the garage door.

Emma enters during the following speech and comes downstairs

Peter tries to signal to Polly that Emma has entered

Polly At least he's well beyond Charity in reading. If I were Emma and Charity was my daughter I'd be a tiny bit concerned. She was trying to read *The Ugly Duckling* to me the other day and do you know, that child is definitely illiterate.

Peter (*trying to cover the mutual embarrassment*) Hello, Emma. We were just saying, what a marvellous painting of Robin.

Emma It's a potato, you fool.
Peter (*peering at the painting*) So it is.

During the following, Emma bustles round the kitchen in a disorganized way gathering up a box of Kleenex, a bunch of beribboned party favours, etc. En route she picks up the bundle of envelopes and the package enquiringly

Polly Birthday cards. Afternoon delivery. (*She goes to pour herself a glass of sherry*)
Emma (*putting them down and moving on*) You haven't seen Jessica Mitchell's Teddy anywhere, have you? It's called Buttercup.
Peter How's the riot in Cell Block Eleven going?

Emma gives Peter a freezing look

Emma We're coping. Or we will be when the conjurer turns up—he was supposed to be here half an hour ago.

Peter finds a Teddy-bear for her inspection. Emma pauses to examine it closely for a moment

Peter Ah, Fred.
Emma No, that's the Honourable Edward Normanton. (*Still bustling around*) Scissors—scissors . . .
Polly Is Matthew behaving himself?
Emma (*sweetly*) He's reading again. All by himself in a corner. I do admire Matthew, bless him, he's so self-sufficient. The rest of them are joining in a game. Hunt the thimble.
Peter I give that about thirty seconds.
Emma (*producing a thimble*) Much longer than that. I haven't hidden it yet. (*She notices a bowl on the table*) Oh, God! The whipped cream! (*She thrusts the bowl into Polly's hands*) Polly, be an angel. (*Taking Polly's sherry glass she knocks it back herself*) Do help yourself, Peter.
Peter No thanks. It's time I wasn't here.

Polly gives him a sharp glance

Emma Thanks for dropping in the tables. I'll get the girl to put them up.
Polly (*to Peter*) Surely you've got time to do that.

With ill-grace, Peter sets up one of the card tables

Emma Is the Bistro still keeping you hard at it?
Polly He's always hard at it, aren't you, darling?
Peter (*defensively*) We did twenty-eight covers last night.
Emma You must have your hands full.
Polly (*standing at the table*) He's got his hands full all right. Haven't you, darling? He didn't get home until two-thirty this morning. The Bistro closes at twelve. (*She starts to whisk the cream*)
Peter I was home at one-thirty.
Polly (*wearily*) Two-thirty. I looked at the clock.
Peter (*heatedly*) It was after two before I could get the last table to leave. At a quarter to two they were ordering *crème-de-menthe frappés*. Regular customers. Monthly account. I couldn't throw them out.

Polly You haven't got any regular customers. You're the one who buys *crême-de-menthe frappés*—for everybody! Anybody who's in the Bistro at closing time gets a *crême-de-menthe frappé* on the house.

Peter I'm trying to build up a clientèle—I've got to socialize.

Polly There's more to socializing, Peter, than sitting down with the customers giving them free *crême-de-menthe frappés* and telling them a very old joke about a nun in a railway carriage.

Peter It's a very funny joke.

Polly You don't tell it very well.

Emma Does my gourmet husband still come in?

Peter He drops in. Have you seen him lately?

Emma He drops in.

Polly I thought he'd be "dropping in" today. Hasn't he bought Adam a birthday present?

Emma If I know Robin he'll be dashing round the toy shops at this very minute. He'll think it's Charity's birthday instead of Adam's. He'll come in, late as usual, with an overpriced, oversexed walking doll that laughs, cries, closes its eyes and urinates. (*Suddenly switching mood, she waves the party favours*) Aren't these pretty?

Peter Well, if there's nothing else you want me for—I'm double parked among other things. (*He moves to the windows*)

Before Peter can get out, Mavis Pawson, the mother's help, appears on the landing and calls over the stairs

Mavis I say! Mrs Partridge! Is it all right for that little lad in the bow tie and glasses to tear up your Charity's reading books?

Polly (*leaping up*) Matthew!

Polly thrusts the bowl of cream which she has been whisking into Peter's hands, thus preventing his exit. She rushes up the stairs past Mavis. Peter, with a heavy sigh, starts whisking the cream

Polly exits

Emma All right, Mavis.

Mavis And your Adam's just said that word again. He said he wants his effing tricycle.

Emma I don't want him down here, Mavis. Tell him I'll bring it up in a minute.

Mavis And that little kiddie that's dressed as a goose is crying.

Emma (*harassed*) In a minute, Mavis. (*She picks up a tray of party fancies*)

Mavis turns to go

Mavis! Here. You can save me a journey.

Emma hands the tray of party fancies to Mavis

Mavis That Marie Louise Whatsernames just swallowed a tooth.

Emma Well, it won't hurt her.

Mavis I know, but the lad it belongs to wants it back.

Mavis exits upstairs

Mavis Hey! Get off that polished table, all of you. (*The door slams behind her*)

Peter (*intrigued*) Quite a female Jeeves. Where did you get her?

Emma (*continuing to tidy the dresser and table*) The agency. It was either Mavis or a Turkish girl with a moustache. She's quite nice, really. She comes from Burnley.

Peter (*politely*) Oh, yes?

Emma And she's wonderful with the children. But the curious thing is that ever since she's been here—what, three and a half, four months? —I've never known her to take a bath.

Peter Never?

Emma Never.

Peter She must do. She'd pong to high heaven.

Emma But when, Peter? She doesn't bath in the morning. She doesn't bath in the evenings. She doesn't bath at weekends.

Peter Holidays?

Emma (*bitterly*) I can't afford holidays.

Peter Afternoons. While you're out?

Emma With two children to watch? They'd drown her. I'm not saying she isn't clean. She is. Scrupulously. She can't wear a dress for two minutes without scrubbing it. But she never ever takes a bath.

Peter But she must have some arrangements.

Emma Perhaps she hoists herself up and sits in the sink. But why no wet towels?

Peter Point. Has Robin met her? What's his theory?

Emma Oh he reckons she pops up the road to the five-minute car wash.

Peter (*giving the idea some thought*) Possible. You still discuss domestic affairs then? When he drops in? I thought you were past that stage.

Emma Did Robin say that?

Peter He has touched bitterly upon his marital affairs being neatly parcelled and handed over to the legal Johnnies.

Emma That wasn't my idea.

Peter Robin doesn't seem to think it was his.

Emma (*defending herself*) I *had* to go to a solicitor, Peter. I mean, if we were going to be really separated it seemed the only thing *to* do. I mean, it seemed more civilized than arguing out the sordid details ourselves.

Peter It's not me you've got to convince, love. It's your husband who thinks he's being screwed for every penny he possesses.

Emma But he isn't! All I want is—well, what I can get.

Peter Precisely.

Emma Why not? He did walk out of the house and leave me with an electricity account, the rates every quarter and two growing kids. What did he expect me to do? Go to the Marriage Guidance Council?

Peter It's a far cry from the Marriage Guidance Council to counsel's advice—which is what you'll end up with from Sutton Boot and What's-their-names?

Emma Sutton, Boot and Sutton.

Peter Once you put your affairs in the hands of a lawyer, Emma, you're hovering on the threshold of the divorce courts.

Emma I never even think of Tom Sutton as a lawyer. He's more of a friend.

Peter So I've been given to understand.

Emma And what's that supposed to imply?

Peter It's only what I've heard. That he's been, well—popping round here quite a bit.

Emma Honestly, Peter, you've got a mind like a Billingsgate sewer! You jump to the worst possible conclusions! Is it inconceivable that a man and a woman can have a perfectly ordinary decent friendship?

Peter I didn't say anything. It's not my business. (*Pause*) Is there a Mrs Sutton hovering in the background?

Emma Tom's a widower. His wife died over— What does it matter what he is! It wouldn't make the slightest difference if he was a raving queer! He's a friend, that's all! Just because *you* can't look at a woman without mentally stripping her down to her suspender belt. Tom's been very kind, and that's all that matters. He's been marvellous to me, and what's more important he's been marvellous to the kids. I don't know how I could have managed without him—he's taken them everywhere. Picnics. The Tower of London. And he's always taking them to the zoo.

Peter Yes. Robin mentioned those trips to the zoo.

Emma Does he approve?

Peter He said it was a case of a man seeking his natural element.

Emma But he's never even met Tom! He's not jealous is he? No—I only wish he was. Do you remember when he knocked that Cypriot waiter down, just for pinching me?

Peter I remember very well. It was one of my waiters.

Emma And Polly emptied a bottle of Vichy water over him to bring him round. We used to have such good evenings the four of us. Getting quietly stoned on *crême-de-menthe frappés*. Coming back here for coffee.

Peter It's not been much fun for any of us since those evenings broke up. Robin still has the corner table. All he does nowadays is argue about the bill. He's convinced you're driving him to bankruptcy.

Emma Oh. The maintenance.

Peter He was chatting about disembowelling your solicitor the other night. He got so heated he knocked over a carafe of *vin ordinaire*.

Emma A large carafe or a small carafe?

Peter I'm not with you.

Emma You know what I mean. Was he alone?

Peter Oh, I see. (*Glibly*) A very small carafe. He was quite alone.

Emma It's true then? That he's not with you-know-who anymore?

Peter (*feigning innocence*) You-know-who who?

Emma *You* know who, Peter. Has he thrown her out?

Peter I—er—tend rather to keep out of all that. Being a friend of both of you.

Emma I heard that he had. She was too much for him, I gather. Poor Robin. Does he mention me at all?

Peter Emma, when your husband comes into the Bistro, as far as I'm concerned he's a medium-rare *entrecôte* and a very small carafe of *vin ordinaire*.

Emma Has he said anything to you about wanting me to take him back?

Peter Usually followed by a *crème caramel*. I get the impression he misses your puddings.

Emma So he does want me to take him back?

At which point Polly appears on the landing

Polly Emma, you know that bottle of stain-remover on the bookshelf?

Emma (*wearily*) Yes.

Polly Is it poisonous?

Emma (*again wearily*) Who's been drinking it?

Polly Well, I thought it was gin. You'll have to come up. That boy who's dressed as a goose wants to spend a penny and I've jammed his zip. Please come, it's sheer murder.

Emma (*going up the stairs*) What's Mavis doing? Can't you organize a game?

Polly I thought you'd organized a game. Oh and you know that thimble you haven't hidden yet—they found it!

Emma Surely I can leave them for five minutes . . .

Emma and Polly exit, and the door closes on the two bickering women

Peter rids himself of the bowl of cream which he has been whipping furiously, and puts it on the dresser. He shakes his hands with exhaustion and turns to leave

At this point Tom Sutton enters through the french windows carrying a large, live white rabbit. He is wearing pin-stripe trousers and a black jacket. He plumps the rabbit into Peter's hands

Tom Good afternoon. Just hold this a minute.

Tom exits

Peter, who has never seen Tom in his life before, looks after him and then down at the wriggling rabbit in amazement

Mavis enters and scurries downstairs

Mavis (*cheerily*) Norman Mendelssohn's just been sick. He hasn't even had his tea yet. (*She searches through the contents of the oddments drawer* *of the Welsh dresser*) I've come down to get the pliers. Only if they don't get that little lad out of his goose costume he's going to have an accident.

Peter studies her with keen interest

Peter Do you like working here, Mavis?
Mavis It's all right. Not too bad.
Peter Mrs Partridge was saying you come from the North.
Mavis I come from Burnley.
Peter So I was given to understand. Funny how there's still this big difference between north and south. I mean, whereas we usually have our dinner at night. Northerners usually have their dinners at—well—lunch time.
Mavis We have our dinners at dinner time. One o'clock.
Peter Exactly. And whereas we normally take our baths in the morning I believe Northerners take their baths in the evening.
Mavis These are them. (*She holds up a pair of pliers*)
Peter Oh good. Although I believe some people take their baths in the afternoon? Miners and so on—D. H. Lawrence covered in pit dust, zinc baths, kitchen range, jugs of hot water. What a grand life.
Mavis I wouldn't know, my father's a traffic warden.

Mavis is about to go upstairs. Peter thrusts the rabbit in her arms

Peter Mavis! Take this, would you?
Mavis What do you want me to do with it?
Peter It's a birthday present for Adam, I suppose.
Mavis (*going upstairs*) He won't have it for five minutes. He had a tortoise once and that ran away.

Mavis exits. Tom enters. He carries a large, bulging suitcase and a gaudy piece of conjuring apparatus—a plywood cut-out model of a house. The suitcase is brightly painted with the words "Mr Lollipop"

Peter Oh dear. Mavis!
Tom Has it escaped? (*He puts the apparatus on the table*)
Peter I thought it was an ordinary civilian rabbit. I sent it upstairs.
Tom (*fiddling with the apparatus*) Not to fret. It's quite domesticated. The kiddies love it. It'll eat out of their hands. Watch for Percy Pussy-Cat.
Peter I beg your pardon?
Tom He's supposed to pop up, but I've given it a bit of a knock. I'm not sure if it's going to work. Watch for Percy Pussy-Cat. (*He presses a lever at the back of the apparatus and a large painted plywood dog flies into view*)
Peter (*with near childish delight*) There he is!
Tom Correction. Percy Dog, I should say.
Peter Percy Puppy?
Tom You've got it.
Peter Do you do much of this sort of thing?
Tom (*cheerfully*) Not a lot. Not much. No. (*He releases the lever and Percy*

Puppy bobs out of sight) Here's a good one. (*He clumsily tugs a large flower bouquet from his sleeve*) It's fascinating, isn't it? It's made out of feathers you know. It baffles me how they think them up. (*Nodding upstairs*) How many of them are there up there?

Peter About fifteen. One of them's come as a goose.

Tom That's not insuperable. Do you know what the secret is? Talk down to them. Now the psychologists say, *don't* talk down to them. Utter clap-trap. You're not telling me that a five-year-old child is on the same mental wave-length as you or I? Ridiculous. (*In a hectoring, patronizing voice, he rehearses his act*) Now then, kiddies, watch Mr Lollipop. Mr Lollipop's got some sweeties. But there's only sweeties for those kiddies that are as quiet as little mice. Now then, let's all be little mice. What does a little mouse do? It sits down.

Peter sits down as though mesmerized

Now then, kiddies, I'm going to tell you about a little friend of mine. And do you know what his name is? It's Tommy Pussy-Cat. As you were, it's Percy Puppy. Now then, kiddies, Percy Puppy lives in this little house. (*He presses the lever and nothing happens*) I'll go to Aitch! Damn and blast the blithering thing! It was working a minute ago.

Polly enters and comes downstairs

Polly Peter, can *you* do something? Some idiot's given Adam a rabbit and the damn thing's jumped out of the window.

Peter What can I do?

Polly Anything! Matthew's crying his little heart out. You know how attached he is to the Flopsy Bunnies.

Peter Why do you sentimentalize him? It's not a Flopsy Bunny, it's a perfectly ordinary common or garden dinner-table rabbit!

Tom It's a highly sensitive pedigree Dutch Angora!

Polly (*to Peter*) Go and look for it.

Peter It'll be half way across Hampstead Heath by now.

Emma enters and comes downstairs, carrying a book

Emma I shall strangle that spotty girl's mother with piano wire. (*She gives Tom a tired smile*) Hello, Tom.

Tom Fully coping, are we?

Emma I don't think you've met—Peter and Polly Butler. Tom Sutton.

Polly So you're Tom. Emma's told me so much about you.

Emma That bloody woman! Of all the presents she could have brought for Adam, she had to fetch him this!

Peter (*taking the book*) *Victoria Plum and the Naughty Elf*, by Mervyn Liversedge. Matthew's read its predecessor, *Victoria Plum and the Magic Penny*. He thoroughly enjoyed it.

Polly You mean *you* thoroughly enjoyed it.

Peter I wasn't wild about the plot but the characters are fun.

Emma You know who publishes this drivel, don't you?

Polly Robin. At least it's successful drivel, darling. A much safer bet than that pop-up Bible he did last Christmas.

Emma (*snatching the book back and opening it at random*) "Victoria Plum was unhappy . . ." How the hell can a plum be unhappy? How can you expect children's minds to feed and nurture on the adventures of a bloody damson? *I* won't have the stuff in the house. (*She tosses the book aside and turns to Tom*) Where's the conjurer, Tom?

Peter I thought *he* was the conjurer.

Emma (*wearily patient*) This is Tom *Sutton*, Peter. My solicitor.

Tom (*to Peter, producing a card*) I had you fooled, didn't I? My card. The number written in Biro is my personal private one. For after business hours. Drunk in charge, common assault—we handle most contingencies. (*To Emma*) As for the conjurer, Emma, he can't come.

Emma He's got to come! There'll be a full-scale mutiny!

Tom He's had to cancel all his bookings. He's been exposed to measles.

Emma Who's going to explain that to the horde upstairs? They wouldn't care if he had bubonic plague. They're thirsting for blood!

Tom Hang on a sec. I've left Adam's present in the car. The show will go on, Emma. I've spent the morning with the conjurer.

Emma Tom, you can't?

With a flourish Tom clumsily produces a string of silk flags from his sleeve

Tom Voilà!

Tom exits through the french windows

Polly Oh, my God!

Emma To think I could have had them in a nice long line at a cartoon cinema.

Polly He'll probably do it very well. He seems quite capable.

Peter (*with a grimace*) Yes—well—if everything's under control, I'll be toddling along.

Emma Everything isn't under control!

Polly Shut up, Peter!

Mavis appears at the top of the stairs and holds up two halves of a broken pottery figure

Mavis Mrs Partridge, can you come up for a minute?

Emma (*angrily*) No!

Mavis disappears hastily

Peter, are you any good at magic?

Peter Who? Me?

Polly You could do them your disappearing act. He disappeared until three in the morning on Wednesday.

Peter Two.

Polly Three!

Emma I can't have Tom here when Robin turns up.

Peter Why not, for heaven's sake?

Polly Don't be a complete fool, Peter. Obviously she can't.

Emma (*taking offence*) What do you mean, "*obviously*" I can't?

Polly (*uncomfortably*) Well—obviously.

Emma and Peter round on Polly. Peter echoes Emma's previous remarks to herself

Peter Honestly, Polly, you've got a mind like a Billingsgate sewer!

Emma There's nothing obvious about it.

Mavis again appears at the top of the stairs and waves agitatedly

Not now, Mavis!

Mavis disappears

Tom is no more than a friend!

Peter He's your friendly neighbourhood divorce dispenser.

Emma He's a solicitor. That's all. He's my solicitor. And that's the only reason I don't want Robin to meet him.

Peter What Emma's trying to say is that she—er—doesn't want Tom and Robin to have a punch-up in front of the kids.

Polly It might be an improvement on the conjuring.

Emma I'm sorry, Polly, but please, please help me to get rid of Tom. He'll spoil everything.

Polly I'm sorry, Emma. Of course I'll do everything I can.

Tom enters with an expensive pedal car with every possible accessory

Emma (*overwhelmed*) Tom!

Tom How about that for a birthday present?

Polly (*to Peter*) That puts your polythene football in the shade.

Tom Of course, I didn't pay the list price—I've got this client in the trade.

Emma Tom, it's absolutely super! Adam will go absolutely potty! (*She hugs him*) You are kind.

Tom It's time I got the floor-show started. (*To Peter, indicating the conjuring apparatus*) Could you give me a hand with the paraphernalia?

A long-suffering sigh from Peter

Emma (*embarrassed*) Oh. Yes. Er—we've been talking about that, Tom. And the thing is—what with the games and the tea and the presents—well—I'm wondering if we've actually got time for the conjuring.

Polly (*emphatically trying to help*) So am I!

Tom (*disappointed, looking from Polly to Emma*) Oh.

Peter Well, you've got to entertain them somehow.

Tom Exactly.

Mavis again appears and this time races downstairs leaving the upstairs door open

Polly recognizes a complaining voice in the babble upstairs

Polly That's Matthew. (*She hares upstairs*)

Polly exits, closing the door

Mavis hurries to a cupboard and searches through it

Emma What is it, Mavis?

Mavis ignores her

Mavis, I'm speaking to you!

Mavis turns and glares balefully at Emma

Mavis It isn't fair, you know. I came here to look after two kids—not the tribe of blinking Israel.

Mavis fishes a large hammer from the cupboard and goes to the stairs brandishing it menacingly

Mavis I'm not kidding, I'll brain the lot of them before I've finished.

Emma Mavis! What are you going to do with that?

Mavis I'm going to clear them all out of my bedroom. They shouldn't be playing dressing-up games in there.

Emma There's nothing wrong with dressing-up games.

Mavis Two of them's got my polka-dot dress on and Norman Mendlessohn's jumping about in my best skirt.

Emma Tell them to take them off at once.

Mavis I've told them. They won't.

Emma Well, make them!

Mavis How can I? They're in the wardrobe.

Emma Get them out of the wardrobe!

Mavis (*brandishing the hammer*) What do you think I'm going to do with this! They've locked themselves in!

Mavis charges up the stairs and exits as Polly enters and rushes down, bent on some mysterious errand. Polly leaves the upstairs door open and the noise is frightening

Polly Dishcloth?

Emma points to the dresser

Polly snatches up a cloth, hares upstairs and exits

Emma watches her go

Emma (*tragically*) I wanted it to be like *home* when Robin gets here and it's turning into a bloody asylum!

Tom I'll settle them down, Emma. They just want a focal point for their natural exuberance.

Peter You'll either have to entertain them or chain them up (*To Tom*) On with the motley then. (*He picks up some of the conjuring apparatus and now sets off upstairs.* (*To Tom*) You're on in five minutes. It'll be like playing the Glasgow Pavilion second house, Saturday night. (*To the children, as he gets to the top of the stairs*) Quiet!

Peter goes out, closing the door

Emma Tom.

Tom pauses

You can't stay. Robin's coming.

Tom So you said.

Emma He is entitled to.

Tom He was entitled to turn up for Charity's birthday but he didn't.

Emma He was away at a publisher's conference.

Tom So he sent her a tin of toffees and the collected works of Charles Dickens—trade price.

Emma They're very useful. She builds houses with them. He did come round the next night.

Tom We know he did. He staggered in at ten o'clock, woke her up and tried to read *Dombey and Son*. And he had hiccups. The man's not cognizant of parental responsibility, Emma, coupled with which he's been having it away rotten. Let me slap a divorce petition on him. Let me do him.

Emma No, Tom! (*She shakes her head*)

Tom How long is it since he had the kids for a weekend?

Emma He took them out only last Saturday.

Tom Yes. To the Business Efficiency Exhibition.

Emma He thought it was the Boat Show. Anyway, the children loved it. One of the computers told them a story.

Tom Where's he taking them next weekend?

Emma Well—nowhere. I promised them a day in the country.

Tom Why can't he take them?

Emma He gets hay fever.

Tom He gets vertigo in the GPO tower and sea-sick on Regent's Park Canal. Any excuse to evade his parental responsibility. He neglects those children, Emma, and what's worse he deprives them financially. You know I've got him in the County Court next week.

Emma Oh Tom, not again!

Tom There's eighteen pounds twelve and a half pence outstanding on a doctor's bill. He's had a final demand.

Emma I know what that is, Tom. It's tonsils. Robin doesn't believe in tonsils. I told you that I'd pay it.

Tom You're not paying it. We'll do him for it. I've got a writ here. And as for that shyster firm of solicitors he's seen fit to represent him . . .

Emma Carling, Hayes and Freemantle.

Tom Carling, Hayes and Freemantle. The whole triumvirate should be disbarred from legal practice. Freemantle to my proven knowledge has issued slanderous statements concerning myself on frequent occasions—the man is an under-handed, double-dealing, pig-ignorant berk!

Peter appears at the top of the stairs

Peter Ready when you are! We're all sitting comfortably.

Emma Can you read them a story or something?

Peter I know—I'll tell them a joke!

Peter goes out, closing the door

Tom (*cheerily rubbing his hands in anticipation*) Well, Emma, let's get the show on the road.

Emma (*flustered*) We've already decided against the conjuring.

Tom They've got to be entertained somehow.

Emma I'll think of something. Anyway, it's time you went.

Tom Where? Why?

Emma I've told you a thousand times. Robin's coming and I don't want you to meet him.

Tom For goodness sake, why not?

Emma Because he'll go spare if he finds you here, that's why not.

Tom I do happen to have your interest at heart, Emma. I have negotiated every single penny of your maintenance.

Emma You've done it for the kids, Tom. And I appreciate that. But you're driving Robin into the workhouse. It isn't fair—on him.

Tom It's what he deserves! Deserting you. Committing adultery. Under the judicial principals of early Christianity the man would have had both his hands chopped off.

Emma If you must know, Tom, there's a good chance he may want to come back.

Tom A reconciliation? I'm sorry, Emma. We can't wear that. We shall continue to pursue our policy of screwing him for every penny he's got.

Emma But I don't want Robin's money, Tom! If Robin really wants to come back I'd rather have Robin.

Tom I refuse to consider it.

Emma Tom—I'm trying to run a children's party. Will you please, please go!

Peter enters upstairs

Peter Come on, old son, it's like bedlam up here. I've told them the one about the nun in the railway carriage—it didn't go down at all well.

Peter exits

Emma I knew it would be like this. My stars in the *Daily Express* said it'd be like this. (*An idea forming*) All right—Tom. Supposing I *did* ask you to be the conjurer.

Tom I am the conjurer.

Emma Yes, but I mean *just* the conjurer. When Robin turns up. Can't you forget you're my solicitor—just for the afternoon? Let Robin think you're the conjurer.

Tom You're sure you wouldn't like me to be the gardener, or the man who's come round to read the gas meter?

Emma Tom, please!

Tom "Mr Lollipop—this is my husband. Robin—this is Mr Lollipop." Yes, I can see that story going the rounds in the Wig and Pen Club. And what am I going to do if he sticks ten pounds fifty in my hand? Touch my cap to him?

Polly enters

Emma He isn't paying you. I'm paying you.

Tom Thank you very much.

Emma Tom!

Polly comes downstairs, carrying a child's goose costume

Tom (*picking up his suitcase*) Damn it all, Emma, I'm willing to do most things for a client, but when you ask me to cloak my profession under the auspices of the Hampstead Magic Circle—well, it's a bit bloody much!

With which Tom goes up the stairs, exits, and slams the door behind him.

Polly, who has overheard the end of the quarrel, looks to Emma for an explanation, which is not, however, forthcoming. Polly decides on a tactful change of subject

Polly We've got the goose thing off Nigel at last. There was an emergency exit where it's supposed to lay the golden eggs.

Emma (*taking the goose costume and looking at the label scornfully*) Moss Bros.

Polly Anyway, I couldn't have him running around in his little vest so I put him in that brown suit of Adam's. I hope you don't mind?

Emma That's the last I'll see of that. They owe me a pair of wellingtons from last year. Amanda Jacobson arrived bold as brass in Charity's duffle coat. And that reminds me, Polly, you've still got three of Adam's Tee shirts. I'd be better off running Harrod's children's department.

Polly What you need is a cup of tea.

Emma What I need is a stiff drink!

Polly You need a rest. You're looking tired.

Emma So I've been told.

Polly Look, when we've got rid of the horde upstairs why don't we all go out for a nice quiet dinner?

Emma All who?

Polly You and Tom. Peter and me. (*Calling*) Peter! We'll go to the Bistro.

Peter enters and comes down the stairs

Emma I can't. I've got a date.

Peter So have I. I mean, neither can I.

Polly (*to Emma*) Who with? (*To Peter, reacting*) Who with?

Peter Robin, actually.

Emma Robin, actually.

Peter (*bluffing*) That is, he booked a table tonight. And I thought I ought to be there to do the honours. (*To Emma*) I didn't know he was bringing you.

Emma I am still his wife. I didn't know we were going to the Bistro. He told me he'd booked a table at Wheelers.

Peter (*floundering*) Ah! Ah! Ah, yes, I remember now. He's on a fish kick. I told him. "Peppered steaks we can do—*Sole Veronique*, no." It's a question of consumer demand. (*Quickly changing the subject*) I say, that polythene football's gone down a treat, Marie Louise Pollock's playing a blinder in goal. Good lord, is that the time. I haven't even made out the menu yet!

Polly Oh, Peter, do leave off!

Peter (*with injured innocence*) What?

Polly You know you're not going to the Bistro. I know you're not going to the Bistro. Emma knows you're not going to the Bistro.

Peter Oh? Where do you think I'm going then?

Polly I don't know, love. I don't even know where *you* think you're going. But whoever she is—you're not going there.

Peter I am going to the Bistro.

Polly You're staying here, Peter. Let's not have a scene in front of Emma.

Peter We're not having a scene.

Polly We damn well will if you try to walk out of that door. The first thing you can do is take off your coat and do some work. Later on you can help clear up the mess. And after that we're taking Emma and Robin out to dinner.

Emma Polly, would you take offence if I said no?

Polly (*taking offence*) Of course not.

Emma You see, I think Robin wants to talk to me about something. I want to talk to him. We both want to talk to each other. For God's sake, surely we can have dinner alone together!

Polly How long has this been going on?

Emma It's not going on at all. Just hints. Just a feeling. He brought round some ties to be pressed the other day and when he invited me to dinner tonight, he sort of gazed at the washing machine and asked if I knew of a really good laundry. Did you know that he's packed it in with you-know-who?

Polly (*feigning innocence*) Who?
Peter You know who.
Polly (*with exaggerated surprise*) No! He hasn't!

*Peter reacts at his wife's pretence at lack of knowledge of the situation.
Polly grimaces at him from behind Emma's back*

Mavis enters

Emma So—I think he wants me to take him back.
Polly And are you going to?

Emma becomes aware that Mavis has entered and is staring down at them

Emma What is it, Mavis?
Mavis Nothing, only I'm being the conjurer's assistant. I've got to come out here and think of a card. What's them black ones with three round blobs?
Peter Clubs.
Mavis That's it—seven of diamonds. Hey, you know that rabbit? It's out in the street, scoffing a carrot. I've just seen it through your window. Ninety-eight—ninety-nine—ninety-nine—a hundred—coming, ready or not.

Mavis exits

Polly So you are going to take him back?
Emma Yes.
Polly (*studiously examining a dish of sausage rolls on the Welsh dresser*) Do you think sausage rolls are a good idea for starters?
Emma You don't approve, do you?
Polly I think cheese straws might have been better.
Emma (*loyally*) He's my husband.
Peter If you want my opinion——
Polly Which nobody does.
Peter Oh. Well, I think it's splendid news. If only for the sake of the kids.
Emma Why has everything got to be for the sake of the kids? What's wrong with my sake, just for once? Hell, I'm a good mother I hope, but from the moment I staggered out of Queen Charlotte's Hospital with that baby burping up at me I was a doomed woman. We never had a row before the children arrived. And then it started. Pottie training. Thumb-sucking. Night lights for and against. Are golliwogs the symbol of a Fascist Society? We didn't go out for six months and then when we did go out there'd be a message or a telephone call or a loud-speaker announcement: "Will the Partridges please go home, their baby is awake again and won't stop crying."
Peter We were lucky with Matthew, he never made a sound.
Polly He screamed without drawing breath for eighteen months—you snored all through it.

Emma Robin was marvellous. Up in his dressing gown at three a.m. mixing sloppy baby foods in little thermostatic heaters. And he'd come down to breakfast with that lovable, understanding, fatherly grin on his face —I could have smashed his teeth in.

Polly I know. How many marriages have gone down the drain just so a cross-eyed infant could cut a front tooth?

Emma We stuck it out for the sake of the children and then I suppose in the end it was for the children's sake we broke up.

Peter Funny that—it was having Matthew that brought us closer together.

Polly You wouldn't recognize your own son if you saw him walking down the street.

Peter I took him fishing only last Saturday.

Polly And you brought him home drenched from head to foot—for all I know you tried to drown him. (*She moves towards the french windows*)

Peter He got his socks wet, woman—he's a boy. Do you want to bring him up as a consenting adult, or what?

Emma You're just like Robin. He reads *Peanuts* every Sunday and thinks that makes him a child psychologist.

Polly Emma, are you absolutely certain you want to take him back?

Emma Yes.

Polly And are you absolutely certain he wants to come back?

Emma He wouldn't bring me two dozen red roses if he didn't.

Polly When did he bring you two dozen red roses?

Emma He hasn't yet—but he's promised to.

Polly Well, here he is.

Emma Be natural, don't stare at him as if he were the Prodigal son.

Robin enters through the windows, his tie askew, carrying a bent car number plate and two broken roses

Robin Here's a good one for the car insurance company. Cruising up Hampstead High Street. No traffic. Swerved to avoid white rabbit.

Emma Oh, Robin, you haven't run over the rabbit!

Robin Brer Rabbit bounded merrily away towards the Health Food stores. I mounted the pavement, winged a traffic warden and finished up against a pillar-box. (*Suspiciously*) Why do you ask? Was that rabbit a friend of yours?

Emma I've never seen it before in my life. (*Taking the flowers*) Oh, thank you, Robin. I'll get a vase.

Polly How much damage have you done to the car?

Robin Not half as much as I'd like to do the raving twit who let loose a white Angora in Hampstead High Street! Well—everything going smoothly?

Emma Oh, very smoothly. Very smoothly indeed.

Polly Didn't you get Adam a birthday present?

Robin (*to Peter*) Lend me five pence, would you?

Polly Oh, lash out and make it ten. After all, it's only once a year.

Robin This is for the parking meter! Adam's present is in the car. I have

spent three days scouring the West End for something suitable. I have
come up with something long-lasting, instructive and unique. Something
that will give my son many hours of enjoyment.

Polly Oh, my God! The *Encyclopaedia Brittanica*!

*Robin disdainfully ignores her and moves towards the french windows, then
pauses to nibble a sausage roll*

Robin Very good. Who made them?
Emma Mavis.
Robin Ah! Has she had a bath yet, by the way?
Peter Apparently not.
Robin (*handing the car number plate to Polly*) I'll just go and get Adam's
present.

*Robin replaces the sausage roll carefully on the plate and goes out.
Immediately, Tom appears at the top of the stairs, now wearing a badly
fitting tail coat and a stiff shirt-front and carrying a wand*

Tom Emma!
Emma (*in some panic*) Don't call me Emma—he's here!
Tom (*coming half-way down the stairs*) That rabbit hasn't turned up by
any remote chance, has it?
Emma Have you looked in the playroom? It might be mixed up with some
toys. (*Turning to Peter and Polly*) And you two, listen. As far as Robin's
concerned, Tom's nothing more than the entertainer. His name's Mr
Lollipop and he's a professional conjurer.
Peter What about Adam and Charity? Won't they turn Queen's Evidence?
Emma Oh, hell, I'd forgotten the kids.
Tom They won't say anything, Emma. Children have a natural instinct
about these things.
Peter Matthew hasn't.
Emma Matthew doesn't know about Tom.
Peter Yes, he does. Tom took Matthew, Charity and Adam to the Tower
of London. You remember. When the Beefeater sloshed Matthew for
giving bubblegum to the ravens.

Mavis appears at the top of the stairs and calls down to Tom

Mavis Hey, thingy! You know that box with the big question mark on it?
Well, Marie Louise what's-her-name crawled into it and she's disap-
peared!
Tom You see, I've got to have the rabbit!
Emma Oh Tom, use Tibbles!
Tom How the hell can I produce a cat from a top hat?
Emma I don't know! How the hell do you produce a rabbit?
Tom It's a different principle? You try picking a cat up by its ears!
Emma Tom, please go upstairs. (*She moves to the pedal car*) Look, take
Adam his present.

Tom Ah, yes! Let's see what his lordship thinks of this.

Tom picks up the car and exits upstairs, tooting the car horn

Emma watches him go unhappily

Polly Don't worry, Emma. It'll be all right. Matthew won't say anything to Robin.

Peter He'll blab out the whole shooting match. If my son has one quality above any other, he's a born Quisling.

Polly (*hurt*) Peter!

Peter I'm only saying he's outspoken, open and above board. It's better than bringing kids up to be sly and furtive.

Emma Are you suggesting that my children are sly and furtive?

The quarrel is broken as Robin enters, proudly carrying a child's pedal car exactly identical to the one brought in by Tom

Robin How's that for a birthday present?

Peter, Polly and Emma stare at the car and then at one another. Robin starts to take the car upstairs. Emma moves to shout after him

Emma Don't take it in now, Robin—the conjurer's conjuring! We thought we'd have the presents after tea.

Robin pauses on the top landing

Robin I can't wait to see his face!

Robin exits, closing the door behind him

They all wait expectantly

Robin returns, still carrying the car

What time does Hamley's close?

Robin, with heavy resignation, humps the car downstairs again and sets it down in the middle of the kitchen. Peter studiously examines one of Charity's paintings on the wall while Polly and Emma make a great show of setting four card-tables for tea. They continue to do so whenever they have a spare moment, arranging cutlery, tableware, heaped plates of cakes and sandwiches, etc., and finally the birthday cake. By the end of the Act the kitchen will be transformed into a colourful engaging setting for the children's tea party

Polly (*to Emma*) Sausage rolls in the centre, do you think?

Robin I skipped a board meeting yesterday to buy that thing.

Emma (*to Polly*) Make sure you leave room for the cake.

Robin I don't object to missing a board meeting—my son's happiness comes first. I only ask to be kept informed about the more important acquisitions of my immediate family.

Emma (*to Polly*) And one of these little jellies on each plate.

Robin I humped it up three flights of stairs to my flat last night. I humped it down three flights of stairs this morning. I brought it along here anticipating my little lad's reaction. And what did he say? "Got one"—as if it were something at the bottom of a corn flakes packet. What lunatic philanthropist bought him the other one?

Emma (*hastily*) Peter.

Robin (*to Peter*) Thanks very much, chum. Nice to know one's friends.

Polly He knows someone in the trade. He got a discount on it.

Robin How much did you pay?

Peter (*making a wild guess*) Oh—er—twelve pounds?

Robin Forty-two quid that set me back. There's a case for the Prices and Incomes Board! (*To Emma*) And while we're on the subject of chucking our money about, who's the chap in the dickie-front lurking about upstairs? Have you taken a butler?

Emma He's a conjurer.

Robin Is that why he disappeared into the loo when he saw me coming? And how much is he setting us back?

Emma I'll pay him.

Robin I hardly think he comes under housekeeping. I know my responsi-bilities. (*His eye lights on the bundle of letters which Peter brought in. He picks them up*) Ah! Mail call! (*Discarding birthday card envelopes*) Master Partridge—Master Partridge—Master Partridge—And one for Mister Partridge. Oh and a registered package for Mister Partridge.

Polly Isn't it about time you stopped having your mail delivered here, Robin? It only costs ten shillings at the GPO.

Robin (*opening the package*) Don't carp, Polly. Surely I don't have to apply in court for conjugal use of the family letter-box? (*He takes out several exercise-books*) Liversedge's latest manuscript. *Victoria Plum and the Fairy Toadstool.* Just in time for the Spring List.

Polly I can't wait for the review in *The Times Lit. Supp.*

Emma Why don't you publish decent books like everybody else? Why don't you publish Kingsley Amis?

Robin (*opening a bill*) When Kingsley Amis rings the bell on *Jackanory* I'll be glad to make him an offer. (*He passes the bill to Emma*) This seems to be for you. Doctor's bill.

Emma But you pay the doctor's bill.

Peter takes the manuscript, sits on a stool, and becomes engrossed in reading it

Robin (*patiently*) I do not pay for tonsils. Thirty-five pounds fifty—final demand. You've forgotten your catechism again. You pay for tonsils I pay for teeth. I pay the mortgage, you pay the rates. I pay the school fees, you pay for clothing. You pay the milkman, I pay the conjurer.

Emma It's very confusing.

Robin It's ridiculously simple.

Emma It may be simple to you but it's confusing to me!

Peter I say, this is very good! "It was a very special morning for Victoria

Plum. She *was* excited! Victoria hopped off her branch and scampered across the orchard to wake up Arnold Apple . . ."

Polly Arnold Apple?

Robin He's a new character. He acts as a sort of foil for William Pear. (*To Emma, who is quite nauseated*) By the way, what did Charity think of the last one? *Victoria Plum and the Magic Penny*?

Emma She hasn't read it.

Robin Why hasn't she read it?

Emma Because frankly I'd rather she got stuck into the *Kama Sutra*! She's seven years old, Robin! I wouldn't inflict that stuff on a retarded two-year-old!

Peter, engrossed in the manuscript, laughs aloud

Robin You might consider my feelings in the matter! Mervyn Liversedge is a crotchety old devil at the best of times—how do you think he'd feel if he knew that his literary masterpieces were banned in his own publisher's house? He'd be round to Heinemann's before you could say Mr Plod!

Emma He can go where he likes, Robin, *and* take his basket of fruit with him. I am not foisting that drivel on my children.

Robin (*angrily*) You do realize that Victoria Plum keeps your children in comfort?

Emma (*also angrily*) Yes! Augmented, apparently, by Arnold Apple!

Robin (*shouting*) Arnold Apple, William Pear, Suzie Strawberry—do you know how much those characters are worth?

Emma (*shouting*) Yes! About twenty pence a pound!

They glare at each other, fuming

Polly I hear you two are thinking of getting together again?

Robin (*still shouting*) Yes! (*Recovering his composure*) Well, yes and no. Yes. It has been mooted. (*To Emma, casually*) All right for dinner tonight then?

Emma Yes.

Robin Good. I thought about eightish.

Emma Eightish would be fine.

Robin Good. Wheeler's all right?

Emma Yes. Fine.

Robin I know you used to like fish.

Emma Oh, I still like fish. I have it practically every day.

Robin Good. (*He is about to sit in the rocking chair and then, in this new and rather awkward atmosphere, thinks that he had better observe the niceties*) May I?

Emma Please. (*Fervently*) It's your chair.

Robin (*sitting*) Thank you.

At which point they run out of conversation

Mavis enters, belts downstairs and into the larder. She emerges a moment

*later holding aloft a table-knife with a pat of butter balanced on the end.
She rushes back upstairs again. No-one has taken any notice of this*

Emma (*to Robin*) Would you like a drink?
Robin Yes, please.

Emma pours a cooking sherry and hands it to Robin

Emma (*apologetically*) It's only cooking sherry.
Robin (*with appreciative surprise*) Good! Oh, thank you.

Emma pours herself a drink, trying to turn the situation into a little party

Emma How about you two?
Polly No thanks.
Peter Not just at this immediate moment. No.

Robin and Emma sip at their sherry

*Mavis again hares down the stairs with the knife, into the larder and out
again. She dashes back up the stairs and exits, with another pat of butter
on her knife*

This time the others look at her with puzzled interest

Peter It's only a theory, but perhaps she rubs herself down with oil every
night.
Robin Very possibly.
Peter H. G. Wells used to, I remember. Never had a bath in his life.
Robin Not Wells. Bernard Shaw. Published by Constable.
Peter (*rising*) Well—you two have obviously got a lot to discuss, and I've
got a busy day ahead, so . . .
Polly Oh sit down, Zebedee!

Peter resignedly sits again. Another pause

Robin Your cold's better then?
Emma Yes, thanks.
Robin And Charity? Is her cold better?
Emma Yes, much.
Robin (*after some thought*) And is Adam's cold better?
Emma (*enthusiastically*) Mmmmmm!
Robin How's your mother?
Emma She's got 'flu.
Robin 'Flu?
Emma Yes.
Robin Mmmmmm.

Another silence

Polly You haven't asked about the cat.
Robin Do you mind! (*Back to Emma*) How *is* Tibbles?
Emma Still moulting.

Mavis, again carrying the knife, appears at the top of the stairs. They all look at her. Self-conscious of the attention she is causing, she tries to look as if she is not there. She tiptoes down the stairs and across to the larder

Robin Mavis! Exactly what is your intention?

Mavis I'm fetching a bit of butter, Mr Partridge.

Robin Without intending to pry—what for?

Mavis That magic feller says not to worry you, because if everybody gets excited it'll swell up.

Emma What's going to swell up?

Mavis The little lad's foot. He's got it stuck fast in your Adam's pedal-car.

Robin So much for the Kiddi-Kraft Seal of Safety.

Emma Which little boy?

Mavis (*to Robin*) I don't know how he's going to get it out because the pedal's got all twisted. He's screaming the house down.

Emma rushes up the stairs and exits

Peter (*to Robin*) Matthew once got his finger stuck in a shampoo bottle. We had hell's own job to get it out. We had to smash the bottle in the finish—there were bubbles coming up out of the bedroom carpet for months.

Mavis It's your Matthew that's stuck in the car.

Polly and Peter rush up the stairs and exit. Mavis darts into the larder and comes out with the butter dish

I don't think butter's much good. My mother always uses pork dripping.

Robin So long as it's grease: butter, lard, pork dripping, beef dripping. It lubricates the ankle.

Mavis It's not for Matthew's foot this. It's for your Adam's head where Marie Louise what's-her-name swiped him with a ping-pong bat.

Robin shrugs despairingly and pours himself a sherry

Mavis hares upstairs and exits as Emma enters and comes down

Emma There's a lump as big as a duck-egg on Adam's forehead. Matthew's stuck fast and yelling his head off. Norman Mendelssohn wants his na-na. Who does one ring on these occasions?

Robin The Mendelssohn household I suppose.

Emma I mean about Matthew stuck in the car. Is it the General Hospital!

Robin I think it's the Fire Brigade.

Peter rushes down the stairs

Peter Have you got a hacksaw?

Tom appears at the top of the stairs

Tom We do not need a hacksaw!
Peter I need a bloody hacksaw!

Robin looks round vaguely and hands his sherry to Peter

Robin Hold this.

Robin searches through a cupboard as Tom comes halfway down the stairs

Tom You'll ruin the car! We can get him out without a hacksaw!

Polly appears at the top of the stairs and sees Peter with a glass in his hand

Polly I ask you to do something and you stand there swigging sherry! Do you realize that your son is in torment? That Pollock child is trying to pull him out of the car by his hair and she will not let go!

Robin finds a hacksaw and hands it to Peter. Peter rushes up the stairs and Tom hares after him. Peter hands the glass to Polly as he passes her

Peter and Tom exit upstairs. Polly downs the glass of sherry in one gulp and follows them, slamming the door behind her

Robin and Emma are alone again

Robin Is he going to be all right?
Emma Oh, why worry? You know how they bring Matthew up. He bawls his head off if you so much as look at him.
Robin I was enquiring about the damage that has been done to my son.
Emma (*relenting*) Honestly, Robin! You must go up and look at him. His little head's out here. He won't be able to get his cap on for days.
Robin Any tears?
Emma Not one.
Robin He's a tough little beggar. Remember that night he fell out of bed? We were at the pictures. We'd got that drop-out baby-sitter in.
Emma We came home at one in the morning and Adam and the drop-out were sitting here together having a teach-in.
Robin *Tom Brown's Schooldays.*
Emma What was?
Robin The film we'd been to. The Baker Street Classic. We had a blazing row in the seven and sixes.
Emma *Tom Brown's Schooldays.* I said how marvellous Robert Newton was and you said it wouldn't be a bad idea to stick Adam's name down for public school.
Robin You said you were against corporal punishment and sloshed me with your handbag.

Robin and Emma smile at the memory of their own idiocy but the tender-

ness of the moment is spoiled by the entry of Peter, carrying the sawn-off pedal car, and pursued by Tom

Peter You can say what you like. I'm getting rid of the damn thing!
Tom It's not a write-off! It's a body job! (*To Robin*) Good afternoon!

Peter exits to the garden. Tom hastens after him

Emma (*glancing towards the top of the stairs*) I can still hear somebody wailing, I hope it's not Adam.
Robin (*sitting*) Not my lad. He's as tough as old boots.
Emma He's quite sensitive really. (*She starts arranging the room again*)
Robin I've yet to see evidence of that.
Emma He is! He paints. He tries to read. He makes up little songs.
Robin The only song he's ever been known to sing is that commercial about Pink Paraffin. He sits, goggle-eyed in front of the television all hours that God sends. They both do. You name it—they'll watch it.
Emma If you had them under your feet every day you'd be glad that they've got television. Don't you know yet that there are only certain hours of the day when I can sit down with a cigarette and a cup of tea—guaranteed? And that's when they're watching *Blue Peter*, *Crackerjack*, *Dr Who*, *Magpie*, *Black Beauty* or *Clapperboard*.
Robin I know you have them twenty-four hours a day, Emma, but why always T.V.? Why can't they curl up with a good book occasionally, like normal children?
Emma Because you insisted on filling the nursery bookshelves with the complete works of Mervyn Liversedge. And if it comes to a choice between Victoria Plum and television—I'd rather they picked up four-letter words from the Wednesday Play!
Robin What's wrong with good old steam radio? *Children's Hour*. All those Aunties. *Toytown*. (*He hums a snatch of the "Toytown" theme music*) Tiddle-um-pum-pum. Tiddle-um-pum-pum. Tiddle-um-pum-pum-pum-pum-tiddle-iddle-um. Larry the Lamb. (*An imitation*) Oh, Mister Mayor, Sir! Dennis the Dachsund. (*Another imitation*) Achtung, Sweinhund! Ah, Larry, my friend, it is a plan for stealing many cross-hot bun that I have.
Emma *Children's Hour* was taken off twenty years ago. So that's how much in touch you are!
Robin All right then, let them *watch* television! But at least organize some selective viewing.
Emma The last time there was any selective viewing in this house was when you forced them both to stay up until nine o'clock to watch a programme about Emperor penguins. Adam fell asleep, Charity burst into tears, you marched out to the pub. And the only thing I learned was that one piddling penguin looks very much like another!
Robin You have a closed mind!
Emma Of course I have a closed mind! What do you expect me to have! Stuck in this house, day after day, week after week! Nothing to talk

about but Lego cars, who made God, and if a crocodile swallowed a policeman, would it go to prison?

Robin The answer to that is obvious. Anyone who's naughty goes to prison.

Emma Then you should have got ten years for what you did to me!

Robin I have already admitted my mistake!

Emma You stormed out of this house over a stupid senseless silly little quarrel! You knew damn well I was crying my eyes out and you didn't give me a second thought! And incidentally Adam *did* have a cold that day. And if I *had* gone to the Foyle's Literary Luncheon I'd have only had to come home again. He had a temperature of ninety-eight point two.

Robin He always has a temperature of ninety-eight point two! It's the way he sucks the thermometer.

Emma Anyway, there was no excuse for calling me a so-and-so so-and-so.

Robin I know, darling. I regretted it the moment I left the house. I spent half-an-hour in the phone box on the corner trying to ring you up.

Emma Don't lie, Robin! You shot out of here and you went straight round to you-know-who!

Robin (*rising*) Emma, I did not even meet you-know-who until a month after I'd left you. I'd nowhere to go that night. I was literally on the phone for half-an-hour and I couldn't get through.

Emma (*remembering, and stopping work*) No. Polly rang me. She could tell I'd been crying. I couldn't get her off the line.

Robin (*moving to her*) I thought you'd taken the phone off the hook.

Emma I thought *you* were having an affair.

Robin I thought *you* were glad to get rid of me.

A misunderstanding has been breached and, for a moment, they are very close

Then Peter, followed by Tom, marches through the kitchen and goes back upstairs

Robin smartly hands Peter his new pedal car to replace the broken one

Tom (*as they go*) ... Destruction of private property, assault upon a person issuing threats. You're in the mire up to here, dear friend. I'll have you in that County Court so fast your feet won't touch the ground. And I'll tell you something else for your benefit. Next time you make a defamatory statement in front of witnesses, bear in mind who you're up against ...

Tom and Peter disappear upstairs, banging the door behind them

Emma flops in a chair in frustration

Robin Who the hell is that extraordinary person?

Emma Birthday parties! I'd sooner be in charge of a demonstration in Grosvenor Square!

Robin You're tired, Emma, that's all.

Emma There's nothing wrong with me that a good fit of hysterics wouldn't put right.

Robin What you need is a break. How would you like me to take the kids off your hands tomorrow? All day.

Emma All day? You?

Robin Pick them up at nine, brisk walk, then all round to my place for a tongue sandwich. Game of darts in the afternoon, glass of tonic water, read the evening papers—back here by six. How's that suit you?

Emma All round to your place?

Robin They've never been there. They'll like it.

Emma (*awkwardly*) Robin, we've had this out before. I don't want the children to meet a certain person. You-know-who.

Robin Look, Emma, let's put all our cards on the table. And if we're going to discuss Sophie let's call her by her name. Sophie. Sophie Lovelady.

Emma Sophie who?

Robin Good heavens, it's only a name. It means nothing to me.

Emma It's the most ridiculous name I ever heard!

Robin The name is not important. I have booted Miss Lovelady out of my life—lock, stock and worry-beads.

Emma I can't understand how you could bring yourself to live with anybody with a name like that.

Robin I was never actually *living* with her, darling.

Emma Come off it, Robin! I know for a certain fact that she was living in that flat.

Robin (*conceding a point*) We were *sharing* the flat, yes.

Emma Well, if that isn't living together, what is? You're not trying to tell me that you didn't sleep together?

Robin (*weighing his words carefully*) Ah. Well—yes—technically. It's a very small flat. You haven't seen it, have you, darling?

Emma Naturally not.

Robin No. Pity you never popped round, you'd have liked the curtains. Anyway, back to touchy subject. The fact of the matter is that there is only the one bed. When Sophie moved in it was either the bed or the floor for yours truly. So—one thing led to another. Darling, it's all in the past. We had a hell of a bust-up and I kicked her out. Finito. How about it, Emma? Let me take the kids out tomorrow?

Emma There's nothing to stop you coming *here* tomorrow. Come for lunch.

Robin May I really?

Emma If you'd like to. You could stay for dinner. We're having a joint.

Robin I haven't had roast beef and Yorkshire since . . .

Emma Didn't she cook for you?

Robin When pressed she could knock up the occasional endive salad. She was also a firm believer in the nutritive powers of yoghourt. She not only ate it—she grew it. I was always finding it breeding on the back seat of the car. (*Pause*) I *do* miss you, Emma.

Emma Because you're living on your own again?

Robin No. I kicked her out because she couldn't hold a candle up to you. I'll tell you what I've missed: walking into a party and everyone looks round and says, "Who's that stunning girl?" My wife.

Emma They didn't really say that?

Robin You'd be surprised at the number of people who've come up to me and said, "Who's that stunning girl?" And it's been you. As often as not.

Emma Thank you.

The mood is broken by Peter who appears at the top of the stairs

Peter What's good for butter?

Robin Bread?

Peter No, you fool, I mean for a butter *stain*.

Emma (*rising*) What butter stain?

Peter On the carpet.

Emma Peter, not the fitted carpet!

Polly appears at the top of the stairs

Polly I'm terribly sorry, Emma.

Emma You damn well should be! Do you know I paid twenty-eight quid to have it cleaned not a fortnight ago.

Polly The record player?

Robin That's my record player! What's wrong with the record player?

Polly Don't shout at me, Robin. It wasn't my fault. Mavis dropped half a pound of butter on the carpet and a score of kids trampled it all over the room. I didn't see it. I almost broke my arm when I fell on the record player.

Robin Oh my God!

Polly I don't think there's much wrong with it. I mean it's going perfectly. It's just that we don't seem able to stop it.

Tom appears at the top of the stairs wearing a glove puppet on either hand

Tom (*to Emma*) This is absolutely ridiculous! How am I expected to keep a horde of kids interested in Sooty and Sweep when there's Tom bloody Jones belting out the *Green, Green Grass of Home*, and your daughter's leading them all in community singing? It's my opinion that Charity is ear-marked for an early appearance in the juvenile courts. Hello again!

Robin I'll thank you, sir, to keep your scurrilous remarks to yourself!

Tom (*to Emma*) I don't think I've officially met your husband.

Mavis appears at the top of the stairs and calls down

Mavis I hope you know there's all blue sparks coming out of the record player and your Adam's trying to play with them.

Robin rushes up the stairs, barging past Mavis and into the living-room

Mavis The little lass with the spots is trying to catch them.
Emma (*collapsing into a chair*) I give up. I absolutely give up.
Mavis And Mrs Partridge . . .
Emma Nothing else, Mavis. I don't want to hear it. *You* can deal with it! Use some initiative.
Mavis (*indicating Polly*) It's about this lady's little boy. Is it all right for him to go into the front garden?
Peter As long as the garden gate's closed, why not?
Mavis Only he's got no clothes on.
Polly What?
Mavis He's taken them all off.
Polly (*moving purposefully towards the stairs*) I'll break him of that habit. If it kills me, I'll break him of that habit!
Peter (*moving after her*) Don't shout at him! Treat it as normal!
Polly I've given up trying to talk to him.
Peter You'll give him a complex!

Polly brushes past Mavis and charges into the living-room. Peter follows her

Mavis (*after they have gone; addressing Emma conspiratorially*) I didn't know whether to say, but that lad in the little short trousers has pushed all their Matthew's clothes down the toilet. (*She brandishes a miniature bow-tie*) I rescued his bow-tie!

Mavis goes back into the living-room as Robin comes out and addresses Emma and Tom from the top of the stairs

Robin Is there no-one in this house with the simple intelligence to disengage a three-point plug? (*To Tom, coming down the stairs*) I thought you were supposed to be in charge of the upstairs side of things? My son might easily have been electrocuted.
Emma (*rising, nervously*) Robin, this is Mister Lollipop. Mister Lollipop, this is my husband.

Tom shakes hands with Robin, leaving a "Sooty" puppet in the latter's grasp, as—

the CURTAIN *falls*

ACT II

Scene 1

The same. Immediately following

Robin I don't wish to criticize, Emma, but don't you think one big table would have been better than four little tables?

Emma For your information, Robin, I have just spent the entire morning setting out four little tables.

Robin I still think we should make the four little tables into one big table. (*To Tom*) Here, Popcorn, given me a hand, would you?

Emma Robin, I absolutely forbid you to lay one finger on my furniture.

Tom She does have that prerogative. You may have the mortgage but your wife is the sitting tenant. In legal parlance she's got you by the short and curlies.

Robin Will you mind your own business! And what are you doing hanging about down here? Do you expect to get paid before you begin?

Emma He's not doing it for the money, Robin. He's a friend of a friend.

Robin We may be hard up but this isn't Doctor Barnardo's. What's the usual damage?

Tom (*smirking at Emma*) Twenty-five pounds.

Robin Twenty-five pounds! I could have my tonsils out for that!

Tom It's the standard rate.

Robin Twenty-five pounds! That's more than I allow myself for a fortnight's food and petrol! (*To Emma*) Do you realize how much I have left after I've paid your maintenance?

Emma I can't help that. I didn't ask you to leave home.

Tom The onus is on you, my friend. A deserted wife is entitled to the fullest compensation the law will allow.

Robin (*shouting*) What the hell business is it of yours!

Emma Robin, remember the children!

Robin I am remembering the children! It's because of the children that I walk the streets without the price of a suit! It's because of the children that I seem to be paying twenty-five pounds for legal advice from a bloody conjurer!

At which point Peter comes downstairs, pursued by Polly

Peter You're not going to make me lose my temper, Polly, so flaming well belt up!

Polly I've belted up. I might just as well save my breath! Don't blame me if your son grows up into a sex maniac. Like his father.

Emma What's happened now?

Peter Nothing's happened. Matthew's perched quite happily on the sofa ...

Polly Stark naked!

Peter He's wrapped in a blanket!

Polly God knows what's happened to his clothes. I can't find them.

Peter They must be somewhere! They'll turn up!

Polly Marie Louise Pollock and that dreadful Nevinson boy in the short trousers are fussing round him with a toy stethoscope. Emma, they're playing at doctors and nurses again.

Emma Oh, no! Not that!

Peter They're not playing at doctors and nurses, for God's sake! He's a wounded soldier, that's all. It's a perfectly innocent childhood game. They're playing at World Wars.

Polly It's still doctors and nurses! (*To Emma*) You know what happened the last time. At half-term. In the Nevinson's garden. Matthew had his clothes off. Charity had her clothes off. The Nevinson boy in the short trousers was claiming to be a surgeon—God only knows what operations he had in mind.

Robin I thought I specifically made it clear three months ago that Charity was not to play with the Nevinson boy in the short trousers.

Emma I can't choose her friends.

Robin *Why* can't you choose her friends? And what is he doing in my house?

Emma It's not your house. It's my house.

Robin It still happens to be in my name. Despite all the efforts of your crooked, conniving lawyer to swindle me out of it.

Tom A dangerously slanderous statement to make in front of witnesses.

Robin One more crack out of you, Houdini, and I'll ram that Sooty down your throat!

Tom In which circumstances an action for assault would lie.

Emma I thought you were supposed to be entertaining the children.

Tom A very difficult operation. (*Indicating Peter*) With this gentleman cursing and swearing and upsetting the whole schemozzle.

Robin Don't blame it on him if you can't hold your audience. You're incompetent. (*To Emma*) What is he? Is he a small-ad or is he from an agency? Because if so you can ring them up now, and tell them I refuse to pay.

Emma For the last time, *I'll* pay.

Robin Not out of my maintenance. (*To Tom*) Get your box of tricks together and pump off out of it. You can send your account to Messrs Carling, Hayes and Freemantle, my solicitors.

Goaded by the names of his rivals, Tom produces his writ—Emma gestures to him to put it away. Tom goes upstairs—remains on the landing

Polly That's typical of you, Robin. Emma arranges the whole party and you stroll in at the last minute and upset everybody.

Emma We were perfectly organized till you arrived.

Robin I can see you were. One, two, three, four adults and you can't control a handful of kids.

Peter If you can do any better, mate . . .

Robin If I could hold the attention of fifteen hundred able seamen as entertainments officer on a naval frigate, I'm reasonably sure I can keep fifteen kids in order.

Emma How?

Robin I don't know. With a game. Simon Says.

Emma You did your Simon Says last year. At Charity's party. The Grantley-Rice twins went home in tears and my daughter was a social leper for three months.

Peter Perhaps it went down better on the frigate.

Emma You can't talk, Peter. You haven't lifted a finger since you came in.

Polly Oh stop it! We've no right to be down here arguing when at any moment that dreadful Nevinson boy might turn the whole party into a sex orgy.

Emma (*to Tom*) Do go up to them. Please.

Tom Is that the feeling of the meeting?

Robin Oh, go on. Buzz off.

Tom May I have my Sooty back, please.

Robin throws Sooty up to Tom — exits?

(*Disparagingly*) Simon Says!

Polly Thank heaven they're not playing Simon Says. That's what led to all the trouble at the Nevinson's.

Peter It wasn't Simon Says.

Polly It was Simon Says. And they'd no sooner turned their backs on him than he crept up and started tickling them.

Peter That is not Simon Says. It's Grandmother's Footsteps.

Polly It was Simon Says.

Robin You've got the wrong end of the stick as usual, Polly. Look. This is Simon Says. Stand up a minute will you, Peter? (*To Peter*) Hands on heads.

Peter, joining in the game, does not move

Robin Simon Says hands on heads.

Peter complies

Hands down.

Peter does not move

Simon Says hands down.

Peter puts his hands down

Stand on one leg.

Peter does not move

Simon Says stand on one leg.

Peter stands on one leg

Put your foot down—Ah!

Robin starts to put his foot down. Robin points at him

That's Simon Says.

Emma That's O'Grady Says.

Robin It's Simon Says.

Polly Whatever it is, the Nevinson boy took advantage of it. If he'd been ten years older they'd have had it in the *News of the World*.

Robin Oh, I'm with you all the way on the Nevinson boy. (*To Peter*) You know he was the one who taught Adam and Matthew that song, don't you?

Peter (*swaying on one foot*) They didn't understand it.

Emma They've got to learn these things some time.

Robin Why, particularly, have they got to learn that Mrs Vickers had no knickers on a windy day, the wind blew right up . . . (*To Peter*) Put your foot down!

Peter does not comply

Polly This is the most disgusting thing I've ever heard in my life.

Robin Simon Says put your foot down.

Peter does so

(*To Polly*) I'm only quoting your five-year-old son. (*To Emma*) And mine.

Emma Your son! It only crosses your mind once a week that you've got a son!

Robin Now what the hell are you bringing up?

Emma Your attitude towards the children that you brought into this world!

Polly They're all the same.

Peter What have I done?

Polly They stick you in the family way and think they've done you the biggest favour in the world. And that's where their responsibility ends. Full stop.

Peter Responsibility? I've stuck with you through one stupid row after another purely because of responsibility! It's only because of Matthew that you and I are still under the same roof!

Polly You can take your half of the roof, as soon as you wish, and shove off!

Peter It'll be my pleasure!

Robin Don't you fool yourself, chum. You won't get as far as the gate before she's round to some back-street solicitor. Half the roof? You'll be lucky to finish up owning the dustbin lid!

Emma If we lived in California you'd be paying me a damn sight more than you are now!

Robin I wish to God I was in California!

Polly It amazes me, it really does! Is this all that ten years of marriage comes down to? How you can split up the joint account?

Emma That's only the beginning. He even came round one Saturday to split up the long-playing records! All I got out of it was *The Theme From Exodus, Teach Yourself Spanish* and *The Best of Mantovani*!

Robin You kept *Where Sheep May Safely Graze*; and the record player!

Emma It's never worked and well you know it! It's *always* had blue sparks coming out of it! There were *green* sparks coming out of it the night you packed your bags. I distinctly remember because Adam and Charity were listening to *The Teddy Bears' Picnic* while you were banging about upstairs and I was crying. (*Close to tears now*) I was down here. I was eating a marmalade sandwich.

Peter Emma, you're not going to solve anything by raking over——

Emma You keep out of it!

Peter I was only going to——

Polly Emma said keep out of it!

Peter All I was trying to——

Robin Simon Says keep out of it!

And Peter is immediately silent

Mavis, wearing a cardboard party hat, comes downstairs carrying an assortment of other party hats. She plonks them into Emma's hands

Mavis Them's your fancy hats.

Emma (*puzzled*) But these are for the children.

Mavis Your Adam says you've all got to wear them. For the tea party. And you've no need to put a cup and saucer out for me, because I'm off out.

Peter (*to Robin and Emma*) I thought you two were going out?

Robin We are going out. (*To Emma*) Didn't you arrange a sitter?

Emma Shut up, Robin. Mavis, you know we're going out.

As Mavis continues, Emma hands out paper hats to everyone

Mavis Your Charity's tooth-brush is in the doll's house and I've put her clean pyjamas out, so if she goes to bed mucky don't blame me.

Emma What's happened, Mavis?

Mavis And if you're looking for your Adam's slippers that big woolly giraffe's wearing them. He tried to seduce me, that's what happened!

Peter Who? Adam?

Robin (*who is now wearing a cardboard policeman's helmet*) That bloody conjurer! (*He rushes halfway up the stairs and bellows*) Lollipop!

Emma (*faintly*) There must be some misunderstanding.

Mavis Oh no, there isn't!

Robin, acting out the role of constable, produces his diary and pen

Robin Right, miss. I shall require a full statement, in your own words, of exactly what took place.

Tom, wearing a cardboard pirate party hat, appears at the top of the stairs

Tom I can tell you exactly what took place. Nothing took place.

Mavis Oooh, you big liar!

Robin You'll have your chance in a moment, sir. Just let the lady say her piece. Take your time, Mavis.

Mavis I was in the airing cupboard getting Charity's pyjamas and he crept in and bit me.

Robin Did he indeed? And do you wish to press with a charge of sexual assault?

Tom That is a leading question!

Robin I shan't warn you again, Lollipop! (*To Mavis*) Continue.

Mavis He was making breathing noises. He crept in on his hands and knees and bit me. I've got teeth-marks on my ankle.

Robin That seems clear enough. (*To Tom*) Anything to say?

Tom draws a deep breath and addresses the company over the banister as if giving evidence from the witness box

Tom The children's entertainment having got out of hand due to certain unsettling influences—(*he glares at Peter*)—at your son's request I entered into a game of Lions and Tigers. Taking upon myself the role of lion I pursued a tiger, the boy Nigel, up the stairs. I lost the scent of my quarry on the first floor. Hearing a movement in the airing cupboard I stalked my supposed prey, growled and pounced.

Mavis And bit me.

Tom If anything, a token nip.

Robin She's got teeth-marks, chummie! (*Flipping his diary closed*) This is a job for the C.I.D. It's outside my jurisdiction. And you've got the cheek to call yourself a children's entertainer!

Tom (*to Emma*) I think this charade has gone far enough. (*To Robin*) I must warn you not to persist with these slanderous accusations. My card.

Tom produces a business card from the top pocket of his tail coat and hands it to Robin

Robin "Mister Lollipop. Family Fun For Everyone."

Tom This is not my suit!

Tom rummages in his suit—pulls out a conjurer's bouquet by mistake, then finds his card. He hands it to Robin

Emma tries to tip-toe upstairs

Robin "Sutton, Boot and Sutton!" (*He catches sight of Emma trying to tip-toe upstairs*) Where do you think you're going?

Emma There's nobody with the children.

Robin Never mind the children! (*Swinging on Tom*) It's this imposter's activities we're concerned with! (*Dangerously pleasant*) I'm going to write to the Law Society about you.

Emma He was only doing us a favour.

Robin I knew he was a charlatan. I didn't realize that he went under an alias. Mr Thomas Lollipop Sutton. Mr Solicitor in conjurer's clothing. What are you doing on my premises? Apart from worming your way into my offspring's affections? (*To Emma*) Is he looking for a hoard of premium bonds under the floor boards? Because I can assure you, you've got every penny I possess!

Emma (*suddenly furious*) He's here because he's a friend of mine. He's here because he at least is making some effort to help! He's here, Robin, because he happens to be my bloody solicitor.

Polly I know it's none of my business, Emma. But do you think this is quite the day for you and Robin to try and patch things up?

Emma It's the same as any other day!

Peter It's hardly that, Emma.

Robin They're right, Emma. Let's talk about it tomorrow. When we don't have the children gumming up the works.

Emma (*moving upstairs*) But we'd always have the children, Robin! That's why it just isn't going to work! That's what you can't get into your thick, stupid head! They're ours, Robin. Yours and mine. And we've got them round our necks like snivelling albatrosses for as long as we live. If it isn't parties it's tonsilitis and if it isn't tonsilitis it's Charity falling into the compost heap or Adam smashing up the furniture. And it goes on in this house, day in and day out, one long hullabaloo, one great almighty bedlam, every time you open this door! (*To emphasize her point, she flings open the door*)

There is total silence from the living-room

What the hell's happened now?

Emma darts into the living-room

Tom, Robin, Peter, Polly and Mavis stare up at the open door

Emma screams off and then reappears at the top of the stairs

They've gone! The little bastards have broken loose! They're all running wild in the street! Well, don't just stand there, all of you! Help me to round them up before they head for the Heath!

Tom, Polly, Peter, Mavis and Robin, galvanized into action, jostle their way up the stairs to exit

Emma barks out orders as they move past her into the living-room

Tom, Polly, take the avenue end. Peter, Mavis, grab the ones that are heading for the main road.

Robin is the last to arrive at the head of the stairs

Robin, you do a quick detour round the garden and pick up any stragglers!

Robin Will do!

Robin hares out via the living-room followed by Emma who leaves the door open
    A moment later Sophie Lovelady, a leggy nineteen-year-old, peers through the french windows and enters. Surprised to find no one about she crosses and calls up the stairs

Sophie I say! Visitors!

There is no reply. Sophie, puzzled, crosses to peer into the larder

Robin, panting from his run round the garden, enters through the french windows. He runs across the kitchen and calls out as he leaps up the stairs

Robin Mission accomplished! Nothing to . . .

Robin reaches the top of the stairs and comes to an abrupt halt as he sees Sophie come out of the larder

Sophie Robin!
Robin (*hastily closing the door to the living-room*) Sophie! Good God, you'll get me crucified!
Sophie (*moving to the middle of the room*) It's absolutely pointless following me, Robin. I'm not coming back to you.
Robin (*coming downstairs*) You've got a colossal cheek, young lady! In the first place, let's get it firmly established who's following who. And in the second place, on the question of coming back, who left who in the first place?
Sophie If you're not following me, what are you doing here?
Robin Good question. And one that I might very well put to you. This does happen to be my house and I'll thank you to take your leave of it! Get out!
Sophie Your house?
Robin Mortgage-wise, yes! And I am here to attend the birthday celebrations of my five-year-old son. A simple ceremony perhaps: but I doubt that the little chap's happiness will be enhanced by the presence of his daddy's ex-mistress. Get out!
Sophie Don't be so gritty, Robin! That's just how you behaved the night you walked out. In the Bistro. And you left Rupert Scott-Forsythe with the bill when it was our turn to pay. He's gone right off you.
Robin Good! I am not exactly on him.
Sophie Sybil Scott-Forsythe is my best friend in all the world: and Rupert's a teddy-bear. Sybil and Rupert think that you are an absolute bore. They said so.
Robin I thank you for passing on the message. You may relay to your friends, from me, that in my opinion, for what it is worth, they are a couple of teenage delinquents.

Sophie (*picking up a sausage roll*) Sausage rolls! Scrummy! Sybil and Rupert think that you are absolutely devoid of any cool.

Robin Cool? Cool? They were smoking pot, girl! In a public restaurant! Great Jupiter, no-one could label me a square—even at my age I'm not averse to the late-night swinging scene but marijuana at eight-fifteen in a Hampstead eating-house is going just that little bit too far!

Sophie Sybil and Rupert are fun people. They always said that you were totally yukky.

Robin Sophie, I happen to have responsibilities. A daughter of seven whose ambition is to become Horsewoman of the Year and the Three A's Long-Jump Champion. What possible chance would the child have in front of an Olympic Selection Committee if her old man had been arrested in possession of cannabis resin?

Sophie Well, there you go. It's your generation gap, isn't it?

Robin It's not a gap between us, Sophie—it's a yawning bottomless chasm. My lot is pipe and slippers, yours is pot and the jet set. In the years to come you'll find one of your own kind. Age is on your side.

Sophie I've already met someone else, Robin.

Robin Already? Five days ago you were shacked up with me!

Peter enters and crosses downstairs

Peter Mission accomplished. Nothing to——

Sophie Peterkins!

Peter (*seeing Sophie*) Good God! Sophie! You'll get me crucified!

Robin I see!

Peter You can't come in here! I've got the wife upstairs!

Sophie I waited on the corner for three-quarters of an hour, Peter. I thought something frantic must have happened.

Robin And when did this little affair take root? It didn't take you long to jump into the breach.

Peter You walked out on her in the Bistro. It's a perfectly innocent relationship!

Robin Ha!

Peter I gave her a job as a waitress. She was penniless. She was demented after you'd gone.

Robin She was potted up to the eyeballs like the rest of her generation!

Peter Look, Sophie, love. Get back to the Bistro. Robin, get her out of here.

Robin She's your waitress.

Peter It's your house.

Polly enters via the living-room

Polly Emma's having a count-up and—— (*Seeing Sophie*) Who, may I ask, does she belong to?

Peter She's a friend of Robin's.

Emma enters and comes downstairs

Emma enters via the living-room and comes downstairs

Emma Who's a friend of Robin's?
Robin I've never seen her before in my life.
Emma Robin, who is this girl?
Robin She just walked in. (*Pointing through the french windows*) Through there.
Emma She must belong to somebody!
Polly (*to Peter*) Well?

Tom enters via the living-room

Tom (*to Sophie*) What the hell are you doing here?
Sophie Daddy!
Emma Daddy?
Tom (*coming downstairs*) I told you two years ago, my girl, I have no wish to set eyes on you.
Sophie Until I got a proper job. I've got one, Daddy, in an absolutely super restaurant.
Polly (*to Peter*) What restaurant!
Peter Look. There's a perfectly innocent explanation. She's a waitress! I have to employ staff!
Polly You made me a solemn promise, Peter, that you would only employ raving queers.
Peter I *was* going to employ queers. And then Sophie happened to pop in, looking for a job . . .
Emma Sophie? Sophie who?
Sophie Sophie Lovelady.
Emma Robin, kindly explain to me what this girl is doing here?
Tom Sophie Lovelady? What sort of a name is that to call yourself? She's not Sophie Lovelady! She's Margery Sutton!
Emma I don't care who she is! Robin, get her out of my house!
Polly Get her out of that restaurant!
Tom (*to Sophie*) Get out of that ridiculous outfit and into something decent!

Mavis enters and stands at the top of the stairs. She stretches her arms across the open doors, barring the children from entering

Mavis Tea time! They're all here, Mrs Partridge! I've got them standing in a long line! And when they're having their teas you can look after them because I'm off out!
Robin Mavis, you are not going out!
Emma (*hastily lighting the candles on the birthday cake*) Shut up, you! I'll talk to you later!
Polly (*to Peter*) I'll talk to you later!

Tom (*to Sophie*) I'll talk to you, miss, now. You're not too big to go across my knee as old as you are!

Emma Tom! Wait until we've fed the children!

Emma, Tom, Robin, Peter, Polly and Sophie join hands and look expectantly towards the living-room, begin to sing "Happy Birthday" with forced heartiness as—

the CURTAIN *falls*

Between the scenes we hear the sound of children descending to the kitchen, devouring the food, and then tearing upstairs again

SCENE 2

The same. An hour or two later

The children have just been ushered upstairs leaving the kitchen looking as if a tornado has just passed through. Chairs are upturned, the table-cloths are stained and awry, remnants of sandwiches and jelly cling everywhere. Only the birthday cake, or what is left of it, remains in its original position. Tattered party favours, burst balloons and torn paper hats are scattered across the floor

Peter, Polly, Emma, Robin and Sophie are completely exhausted. They are flopped in their chairs, their paper hats perched limply on their heads. Tom is brooding to himself over a plate of trifle. Mavis at the top of the stairs, is ushering out the last of the children. The door to the living-room is open and we can hear the children engaged in a terrific hullaballoo. Mavis screams into the living-room

Mavis SHURRUP! (*There is immediate and total silence*) You're all going to do what I say now and I'll spifflicate the first one that breathes!

Mavis glares triumphantly at the group in the kitchen and marches out, slamming the door

There has been a truce during the presence of the children and now they all find a new lease of strength as they launch into argument. They all speak at once

Emma	Right!	
Polly	(*to Peter*) Now . . .	
Robin	(*to Peter*) I blame you for this girl's presence . . .	*speaking together*
Emma	(*to Robin*) I couldn't say	

anything in front of the children but of all the . . .

This is interrupted by Mavis, who enters at the top of the stairs

Mavis I say!
Emma You keep out of it!
Mavis The mothers are coming! The mothers are coming! And I'm still going out at half-past six, I don't care what you say. And——
Polly Mavis! Get in there and see to those kids before you're on the next train to Burnley with a boot up your backside.

Mavis, chastened, goes out

Sophie I say—has she had a bath yet?

The front door bell rings

Emma (*to Robin*) Is nothing sacred to you? Have you been discussing Mavis's toilet habits with this girl?

Mavis reappears

Mavis That's the door.
Emma Then answer it!
Polly Go on!
Mavis (*defiantly*) I'm still going out at half-past six, you know.

Mavis goes out, slamming the door

Robin That girl has definitely got to go!
Emma Whoever I choose to employ in this house, Robin, is no longer any business of yours.
Polly And while we're on the subject of employment, Peter, I might warn you that I intend to take a closer interest in the Bistro staff. Waitresses! What are you serving these days? Devonshire Cream Teas?
Peter You may not be *au fait* with West End dining habits, Polly——
Polly I'm not. It's over eight months since you took me out. It's ten!
Peter When will I get it into your head that I've got a restaurant to run! You won't come into the Bistro.
Polly Naturally I don't come to the Bistro. I'm never invited to the Bistro. You don't want me to come to the Bistro. If I come to the Bistro I'm likely to come into contact with your latest hobby. (*Glaring at Sophie*) She might even serve me with a pot of tea, a jug of hot water and a buttered bun!
Peter They have waitresses everywhere! I am here to inform you that waitresses are the latest in-thing at every trendy Mayfair haunt!
Polly You're beginning to sound like *What's On?*!
Sophie They've got a lady disc jockey at the Upside Down Place.
Robin She's right, you know! And they've got waitresses there, too.
Peter Thank you.

Emma Would somebody kindly explain to me the Upside Down Place?
Sophie Everyone goes to the Upside Down Place. Pan's People, The
   Young Generation . . .
Emma Thank you. (*To Robin*) You must have had a ball.
Robin I haven't been inside the Upside Down Place. I read about it
   somewhere. (*Inventing wildly*) In *What's On?*
Peter The Upside Down Place has been visited by the Good Food Spy
   and got a write-up in this month's *Nova*. To say nothing of a five-
   hundred-word rave notice in *What's On?*
Robin Thank you.
Peter The Bistro has not, as yet, graced the pages of the *Hampstead
   Gazette*. (*Suddenly furious*) Peter O'Toole lives just around the corner
   and he doesn't even know that I bloody exist! The Bistro doesn't get
   a mention. Anywhere! Although if somebody doesn't get round there
   and open the doors P.D.Q. it might find its way into the obituary
   columns. Sophie, scoot off, give my compliments to the chef and——
Polly You don't imagine, for one moment, that she's going back to the
   Bistro?

*Sophie sweeps up an indeterminate mess from the floor into the large manilla
envelope which previously contained the "Victoria Plum" manuscript*

Peter She works there, woman!
Polly She is not going back to the Bistro!
Emma She's certainly not staying here, Polly.
Robin Certainly not!
Emma Shut up, you!
Peter Sophie. Nip round. My compliments to the chef and tell him that as
   my wife has decided to drive me to bankruptcy, the chicken livers may
   go by the board.
Polly You chose your own path to self-destruction, Peter, when you de-
   cided to open a Bistro specializing in rump steak bang next door to the
   dogmeat shop.
Sophie I'll put this in a dustbin.
Robin (*recognizing the envelope*) Hang on a sec! That's my envelope.
   Victoria Plum was in there.
Sophie She isn't any longer. It's mostly strawberry blancmange now.
Robin There was a valuable manuscript in that envelope. Where is Vic-
   toria Plum? (*He prowls around looking for the manuscript*)
Polly Gone for walkies with Arnold Apple.

Sophie goes out into the garden with the envelope

Tom, having demolished his trifle, puts aside his plate and calls after her

Tom And when you come back, madam, I want a word with you! (*He
   addresses Peter in Sophie's absence*) I'm extremely sorry, my friend, but
   that young lady's waitressing days are over. (*Darkly*) I might even make
   her a ward of court, I haven't made my mind up.

Robin Emma, have you moved Victoria Plum by any chance?
Emma I wouldn't touch Victoria Plum with a bean-stick, Robin.
Robin Be serious, Emma. I've lost a particularly valuable manuscript.

Mavis enters

Mavis Is it all right for Jessica Mitchell to go off with Norman Mendelssohn's na-na?
Emma Yes! Give Norman Mendelssohn's na-na the whole bloody bunch of them! Mine as well! Let's get rid of them all!
Robin Mavis, have you seen Victoria Plum?
Mavis Is she that dark little girl with the ringlets?

Robin throws up his arms in despair

Because if it is, she can't find her coat.

Emma, in exasperation, goes upstairs and exits, followed by Mavis

Sophie enters from the french window

Tom And you can find *your* coat, miss. We're going.
Sophie I haven't got a bally coat!
Tom No, and you've got no bally self-respect either! Walking through Hampstead in broad daylight showing everything you've got!

Robin gives up his search to listen in surprise to this exchange

Sophie How can you talk about clothes when you're three hundred years old!
Tom Yes, and you'll be three hundred years old when I knock you back into the middle of next week!
Robin If that's the way her father talks, I'm not surprised that she changed her name.
Tom I'll thank you to keep out of this! The girl would have been back with me months ago had she not fallen into your clutches! I have not as yet discarded the possibility of an action against you concerning the enticement of a female minor! Don't force my hand.

Mavis appears at the top of the stairs with the rabbit

Mavis I say! The Happy Wanderer's returned.
Robin That bloody rabbit from the High Street.
Mavis The Nevison lad in short trousers found it in the garden, he wants to know if there's a reward.
Tom My best compliments to the little chap, tell him he will be suitably reimbursed.
Mavis (*goes off practising the words*) Suitably reimbursed.

Mavis exits

Robin Wait a minute! Are you the maniac who loosed that vermin on the High Street?
Tom That happens to be a valuable trained pedigree Angora.
Robin I'm going to sue you for the damage done to my car.
Tom (*producing a writ cheerfully*) Litigation is my business, dear friend. Outstanding Doctor's bill, County Court, ten a.m. Monday morning— Belt Blancoed—Boots Polished.

Emma appears upstairs

Emma I'm sorry, Polly, but I've got to ask you to talk to Matthew.
Polly What's he done now? (*She goes upstairs*)
Emma He's trying to wrap up the cat, Polly. In a brown paper parcel. He'll suffocate it. He's got dozens of going home prezzies already. He can't have the cat, Polly, and besides she'll go for him. She's always been marvellous with children—but after all she's only human!

Polly exits

Emma continues to the others

As for that bloody little mercenary Marie Louise Pollock, did *anyone* hear me promise her a box of Leggo to take home with her? It's my belief she sells it secondhand. (*She makes a final appeal over the banisters*) And can somebody look for a child's pinafore with little red dwarfs all over it.

Robin, Peter and Tom listen to this tirade with open-mouthed astonishment

Emma exits upstairs

Sophie runs upstairs

Sophie Coming!
Tom (*calling after her*) And don't think I've finished with you yet, miss!

Sophie pauses at the top of the stairs to put her tongue out at Tom and then nips into the living-room

I'll knock your bloody head clean through your shoulders if you do that to me! (*To Robin and Peter, suddenly deflated*) You'll have to forgive me for adopting that attitude but I was brought up in a strict Methodist home.
Robin I'm only surprised that my wife has allowed you within half a mile of my children.
Tom It's all very well for you to talk, but you've still got it all to come.

You think you've got problems now, but give your kids a year or two and then see where you stand.

Peter I fail to see what you're worrying about. I think she's a wonderful girl.

Tom (*giving him a bitter look*) So it would seem.

Robin (*pompously*) After all, children are only what we make them.

Tom I used to use the very same words myself. I devoted my life to that girl when her mother died. I never remarried, though there was ample opportunity. But no, I made it my duty to build a future for my little girl and myself. I gave her everything. Typing lessons. Linguaphone records. I even coughed up for a well-known West End beautician to remove the surplus hair from her legs.

Robin and Peter display distaste

It was my impression that we couldn't have been closer and then, blow me, on her seventeenth birthday she announces that she's leaving home.

Robin You were the one who let her go.

Peter Turning her out at seventeen? What else did you expect?

Tom Excuse me, friend. I gave that girl permission to leave the shelter of my walls on the strict understanding that she'd be sharing a flat with an old family friend. She also gave me to understand that she would be taking up bona fide employment as a trainee model or a hostess for Aer Lingus. (*With sudden anger*) From that day to this I've not had a bloody word from her! Not so much as a swinging postcard! (*Calmly again*) Imagine my concern when I discovered this afternoon that my daughter has, until recent date, been cohabiting with the husband of an esteemed client. Committing adultery—frequently and habitually.

Robin There's no need to be coarse.

Tom Frequently and habitually. It's the correct legal terminology. It'll be all down in black and white on your wife's divorce petition.

Robin There is not going to be a divorce!

Tom I am acting under instructions from your wife. It's not my decision, I only wish it were. I was giving the matter a great deal of thought over tea. By the time we got round to the pudding course I had reached the opinion that it was my bounden duty to clobber you. But no, I don't blame you—I blame myself. I should have realised that when Margery left home she had entered a state of sexual awareness. One expects your modern teenager to indulge in heavy petting. I expected that. But I credited the girl with more intelligence than it seems she has. (*Again incensed*) Look at her! Nineteen years of age and not the bloody sense she was born with! We can only hope and pray she isn't up the stick! Cohabiting with a fly-by-night and obtaining casual employment as a washer-up in a roadside caff!

Peter Do you mind!

Tom Admit it! Have you set eyes on her insurance cards? I tried to bring her up according to your present-day methods. I listened to the psychological pundits. Give them a free rein, they say. Allow young people to have their heads. Wrong again, psychological pundits. A girl that age should be kept locked in her room, strapped down to the bed. Never mind psychology. I see that now. Well, I shall get out of this monkey suit, I shall drag that girl back home if needs be, and I shall belt the living daylights out of her. I fervently hope it may not prove too late.

And, with a formal bow to Peter and Robin, Tom moves up the stairs with as much dignity as he can muster and exits

The others watch him go

Peter There goes the spokesman for the Dark Ages.
Robin I'm not too sure he hasn't got a point, actually.
Peter What absolute rubbish! You've got to let kids fend for themselves at some point in life.
Robin All the same, I wouldn't like to think that my daughter was trotting round restaurants picking up every *Maître d'* who slapped a bordelaise steak in front of her.
Peter Who brought her into the Bistro in the first place? You were the one who walked out of house and home for her. At least I've got the decency and common sense to keep my indiscretions out of the family fold! I don't break up the happy home for the sake of the odd dolly!
Robin I did not break up my home for the sake of a dolly, odd or otherwise. There were temperamental differences.
Peter I hope you realise that your two kids are looked upon by all their friends as part-time orphans.
Robin You're a great one to talk. One affair after another. Out till all hours every morning. A little lad that hardly knows you from the milkman at the age of five.
Peter My boy will grow up with the benefit of not coming from a broken home!
Robin My children will have the decided advantage of not being brought up in an unhappy atmosphere!

Sophie comes on to the landing

Sophie (*casually*) Poor tiny Adam's crying his heart out.
Robin He's always crying! (*Moving to the stairs*) What's wrong with him this time?
Sophie He says he wants to go and live with a boy called Nevinson and be his new brother.
Robin (*with an embarrassed grin*) Marvellous imagination that boy has! Marvellous!

Robin goes upstairs and exits

Peter Your father's demented!
Sophie He's in a frightful frost! (*She remains on the stairs*)
Peter He seems to think he's got the right to run your life. I'm glad to see you've got the guts to stand up to him.

Sophie He had the cheek to offer me a Lambretta if I gave up seeing you.

Peter I hope you told him what to do with it.

Sophie I said I wouldn't go back for anything less than an Aston Martin.

Peter An Aston . . . Well, I suppose if it's a choice between me and a bloody motor car, that's about it.

Sophie Honestly, you're as bad as Robin at taking offence. I'm definitely beginning to go off older men.

Sophie flounces out in a huff as Emma comes downstairs followed by Polly. They are also engaged in a childish, petulant argument

Polly It's only a Magic Pencil when it's there, Emma! Good heavens, tell me what it cost! I'll pay you for it.

Emma It's not a question of the Magic Pencil, Polly. It just happens to be the way that we've brought Charity up. I'm not concerned with the Magic Pencil. Or what it cost!

Polly I know what it cost. Magic Pencils cost nine pence—in Woolworth's.

Emma They happen to cost eighteen and you get them at Galt's.

Polly If they came gold-plated from Asprey's they still wouldn't be worth the fuss that Charity's making!

Peter What in God's name has happened now?

Emma Matthew has stolen Charity's Magic Pencil. They've been fighting on the landing over it.

Polly He only wanted to borrow it!

Emma He snatched it clean out of her hands. It's Charity's Magic Pencil, and she wants it!

Polly We're not to know that Charity didn't steal it from him. He might have brought it with him.

Peter He did not bring a Magic Pencil into this house.

Polly He might have done.

Mavis enters and gesticulates from the top of the stairs then off

Emma Don't start accusing Charity, Polly. You know very well that Matthew came in here empty-handed. I bought two Magic Pencils for party prizes yesterday—two Magic Pencils and a Crazy-Maze. The Nevinson boy won the Crazy-Maze for Postman's Knock, naturally. One of the Magic Pencils went to the Sandelson girl for Musical Chairs. Charity must have had the other.

Peter (*to Polly, rhetorically*) If it belongs to Charity make him give it back to her!

Polly That's right, Peter, don't stand up for your own son, will you? Matthew is a guest here, Emma! If Adam comes to play with Matthew he shares all his toys. He's very good like that.

Emma We've trained Adam and Charity to look after their toys. They treasure them. It's the way they've been brought up.

Polly To be selfish and possessive? We've taught Matthew to share everything he has. And I might remind you that when Adam came round to us last Saturday, Matthew let him go off with his Action-Man without a murmur.

Emma Adam asked if he might *borrow* that Action-Man, that's quite a different thing.

Peter Hang on a sec. Which Action-Man?

Polly Matthew's Action-Man. Adam took it home with him. The one with the little flippers, yes.

Peter Well, that's charming, isn't it? I only got him that Action-Man a week ago. And I had to send away for it!

Robin enters and comes downstairs

Robin Are you aware that there's a goose sitting in the window-seat stinking the living-room out?

Emma Yes!

Polly It's Nigel. He's done poops. (*To Emma*) I told you not to put him back in that ridiculous costume.

Emma He came as a goose, Polly—he'll go home as a goose. I wish you wouldn't interfere!

Peter She's only trying to help, Emma! You asked her round to help.

Robin Hello? What's started this lot off?

Peter Your son has walked off with Matthew's Action-Man.

Robin Which Action-Man?

Polly Matthew's Action-Man!

Emma He borrowed it, that's all.

Robin This house is full of Action-Men. There's a battalion of them in the nursery and at least three, to my certain knowledge, have invaded the dining-room in tiny parachutes. If you want to be petty, Peter, nip upstairs and take your pick!

Peter I'm referring to a Frogman Action-Man.

Robin Oh, for pity's sake, they're all the same! Action-Men are interchangeable!

Peter Frogmen Action-Men are very difficult to get! I had to write off to the makers for that one and now your son's nicked it.

Robin All right. I'll give you two paratroopers for it. Two paratroopers or a combat sergeant. How's that?

Peter No! I specifically want that Frogman Action-Man. He comes in very useful in the bath.

Robin In the bath?

Peter Matthew's bath, twit!

Robin Don't you "twit" me! If you can be so childish over a little thing like an Action-Man, it wouldn't surprise me if you had your own plastic duck!

Polly My husband is not childish! Your wife began the argument over a silly, stupid Magic Pencil!

Robin Which Magic Pencil?

Peter That Magic Pencil Charity is hugging to herself.

Robin The one Matthew and Charity were squabbling over on the stairs?

Emma Yes!

Robin (*taking a cheap propelling pencil from his pocket*) This Magic Pencil?

Peter How did you get hold of it?

Robin It happens to be mine.

Emma Robin! You haven't stolen that pencil from your own daughter!

Robin I tell you it's mine—it belongs to me! This particular Magic Pencil happens to be my own personal private property! I got it in the toy shop yesterday when I picked up Adam's car.

Peter A Magic Pencil?

Robin Why not?

Emma You'd really do that, wouldn't you, Robin? You'd steal a toy from your own child and then lie about it.

Robin I tell you, it's mine! It writes in three colours. I saw it on the counter in the shop and I thought, "Hello!", I thought. "That'll come in useful when I'm checking proofs." (*Demonstrating with the pencil*) Look—now it's blue, now it's green.

Polly May I see that, Robin?

Robin (*giving her the pencil*) Certainly. It's quite ingenious really. There's little secret buttons all round the top.

Polly (*exploding*) You bloody liar!

Robin I beg your pardon!

Polly (*to Peter*) This is Matthew's pencil! It's Matthew's own pencil!

Peter (*uneasily*) Don't talk rot, Polly. He didn't bring a pencil.

Polly But it *is*! Matthew always nibbles his pencils. I recognize the chew marks round the top.

Robin Those are my chew marks. I was chewing it last night.

Emma That pencil belongs to Charity, Polly.

Polly It does not. I bought this pencil over a week ago. I can show you the very shop.

Peter It can't be Matthew's, Polly. Matthew didn't bring it. It didn't fly here by itself.

Polly I can recognize a Magic Pencil when I see one.

Mavis appears at the top of the stairs

Mavis Mrs Partridge! Your Charity's having a scream fit. And she says she won't stop until she gets her Magic Pencil back.

Emma (*to Polly*) There you are! It *is* Charity's. (*Extending a hand for the pencil*) Thank you, Polly.

Polly (*not letting go*) Mavis, I have reason to believe that this pencil belongs to my son.

Mavis It doesn't, Mrs Butler. It belongs to Charity. Because I was there when she got it. That young lady gave it to her. Upstairs. Because Charity thanked her for it and I heard her say, "Thank you, Auntie Sophie." That's what she said.

Emma Auntie Sophie! (*Swinging on Robin*) Since when did that—that solicitor's daughter become a member of the family?

Polly (*to Peter*) When did she start acquiring my son's pencils, that's more to the point. Mavis. Leave this room and close that door behind you.

Mavis, loath to miss the argument, hesitates

Now!

Mavis scurries out

(*Turning back to Peter*) You gave it to her, didn't you? Admit it?

Peter Admit what?

Emma (*to Robin*) So you did take it from Charity—and lied about it.

Polly Just a minute, Emma. Peter, I want the truth. How did that—that waitress come to be in possession of my child's pencil?

Peter I don't know!

Polly I do. You gave it to her.

Peter I did not give that girl a pencil!

Robin (*to Polly*) You are holding my pencil and I'd like it back . . .

Emma Of all the low-down underhanded paltry tricks, to steal a pencil from your own child . . .

Polly To steal your own son's pencil, Peter, and to give it to some girl! How low can you get? And don't think I've forgiven you for that bottle of scent!

Peter What bottle of scent?

Polly The scent you bought last Saturday. Don't say you didn't—I found the receipt. I didn't mention it at the time because I didn't want to quarrel in front of Matthew. But when you take *his* things—he's five years old!—when you take *his* things and give them to her!

Robin Do you think I might have my pencil, please?

Polly (*ignoring Robin*) What did she give you in return for it, that's what I'm beginning to wonder? (*Holding up the pencil*) If she bestows her favours for a ninepenny Magic Pencil—what would she do for a Parker pen?

Robin (*making a grab at the pencil*) If you've quite finished with my Magic Pencil . . .

Emma (*also making a grab for it*) Don't you dare touch Charity's pencil, Robin . . .

Polly It belongs to Matthew!

Robin I want my pencil!

The four of them tussle for possession of the pencil

Tom appears at the top of the stairs, having changed back into his jacket and pin-stripe trousers

Tom (*calling down to them, jocularly*) Come along, friends! Let's be civilized. Surely we can settle this in court? Who wants to slap a writ in first?

Peter, Emma, Robin and Polly, embarrassed at being discovered in a childish squabble, break apart as Tom comes down the stairs

Emma (*indicating Robin*) I want a divorce from him.

Polly (*indicating Peter*) I want a divorce from him.

Emma With custody of both children.

Polly I want him denied all access to his.

Tom Well, well, well! It's turning into a proper busman's holiday, is this! All present and correct and back in legal uniform. Sutton, Boot and Sutton at your service.

Polly I want to arrange an immediate legal separation while the suit is pending; does that cost extra or is it all thrown in?

Tom One moment, madam. First clients first. I'll come to you in a moment. Emma?

Emma I want a divorce!

Tom We could only do our utmost to get it in the Law Courts Lists.

Emma I want a divorce! I can't wait for the lists. I want to be rid of him now.

Tom Ah, well, there you pose a problem, we might be able to get the hearing expedited, at a push, we'll need to prove extenuating circumstances. You don't have the good fortune to be pregnant by a third party, by any happy stroke of fate?

Robin You are speaking to my wife!

Tom I must ask you to contain yourself, sir, I'm wearing my solicitor's hat at the moment and, by rights, you shouldn't be in this room at all. It comes under the heading of collusion. I could get struck off the lists. Right. Pudding Club stakes a write off as extenuating circumstances. Think again. We're not defeated yet. (*To Robin*) You're not by any chance a practising homosexual?

Robin How about me practising grievous bodily harm on a part-time conjurer?

Tom I shall treat that remark with the contempt it deserves and strike it from the minutes. No, you're not a practising homosexual—far from it. As some of us have cause to regret. If he's not a puffer and you're not in pod, Emma, we find ourselves up the proverbial creek, without an affidavit.

Emma There must be something we can do. He's committed adultery.

Tom I'm sorry, Emma, but the requisite proceedings could never take place under my auspices. There will be no divorce. I'm bottling it.

Polly Bottling it? It's scandalous. I shall go to the Queen's Proctor.

Tom For pity's sake, madam, you're a parent yourself. Try and see it from a parent's point of view! The correspondent in this marital hot-bed turns out to be my own daughter! And whilst being the first to admit she's turned into a proper little whore, I still can't bring myself to drag her through the courts.

Emma But what about my divorce?

Tom I appreciate your predicament, Emma, but as the Bible would have us believe, blood is thicker than water. There is good in that girl. Wilful, yes, she may be headstrong, she may be impetuous, but she has character.

Polly Mr Sutton, I have no wish to be offensive, but you've only got to look at that girl to see that she's been in every bed in the King's Road.

Tom Madam. I have just had a long talk with the young lady in question and I would advise you, off the record, that she has given me her solemn oath that nothing untoward has taken place between your husband and herself. To put it in common parlance he hasn't been there yet. She's willing to swear to that in court—she might be perjuring herself, I don't know—we're all entitled to that loophole in the law. It would be your word against hers—you wouldn't stand an earthly. (*Turning to Emma*) I realize that this may mark the end of a very sincere personal friendship—but there it is.

Robin You would do my wife and myself a very great favour if you would remove yourself and your daughter from this house.

Tom I intend to do that thing—I shan't hang about. The conjurer will call to pick up his paraphernalia tomorrow, at your convenience. (*Turning to Peter*) My humble apologies to you too, sir, for any awkwardness caused, but my daughter's happiness must come first. (*Calling up the stairs*) Margery! Margery! I'm calling you!

Apron off.

Mavis appears at the top of the stairs

Mavis Was that you shouting?
Tom It was.
Mavis Are you wanting that young lady that was here?
Tom I am.
Mavis You'll be disappointed then, because she's gone.
Tom She can't have gone!
Mavis She has, because I saw her going up the garden path. And she told me to tell you that she's not coming back.
Tom Did she say where she was going?
Mavis Where's Tangiers?
Robin Morocco. North Africa.
Mavis That's where she's gone. She says she's going to open a men's boutique.
Tom That's it then. I wash my hands of her. She'll end up in some harem in the White Slave Hell. (*Exploding*) Isn't it flaming marvellous! There's me here, doing my best to avert a scandal, and there's Mary-Ellen hell-bent on getting herself in the *News of the World*! Who'd have kids? I tell you, if I don't finish up a bloody monk!

Tom goes out through the french windows

Mavis calls after him

Mavis (*coming downstairs*) I say! (*But Tom has gone. To the others*) She told me to tell him, it's not her thing.
Robin I think we can safely assume that he got the message.
Mavis (*a gust of anger*) And it's not my flaming thing either!
Emma Mavis!
Mavis (*to Peter*) Do you know how much she pays me a week?
Emma No-one is interested in discussing your wage.

Mavis Ten pounds. For a twelve-hour day and one afternoon off. (*To Emma*) Do you know how much that young lady told me I could earn as a waitress?

Peter Waitresses have to be trained.

Mavis Forty-five pounds. With tips. And meals thrown in.

Peter Rubbish.

Polly Forty-five pounds!

Peter The grossest exaggeration.

Polly (*to Emma*) Do you know what he gives me for housekeeping? To bring up a growing child?

Robin I don't really think this is going to be a very fruitful discussion.

Mavis My mother brought up a family of five on eight pounds ten shillings a week.

Robin And none of you any the worse for it, eh?

Mavis And we didn't have honey and yoghurt for breakfast—we had fried bread and liked it!

Robin By gosh, there's an example to us all.

Emma That'll do, Robin!

Mavis Do you know what your Charity came out with yesterday?

Emma That'll *do*, Mavis.

Mavis Yes, it will do! Because you can have a week's notice. I'm off to be a waitress. (*She runs upstairs*)

Peter I'm afraid there are no immediate vacancies but I shall keep your name in——

Mavis At a *proper* café. Either a Wimpy Bar or a Golden Egg. And if any of your kids—*any* of 'em—so much as show their noses round the door, they'll get a brunchburger right up the bracket.

Mavis exits slamming the door

Polly (*swinging on Peter*) Forty-five pounds a week!

Peter She's got it all wrong!

Polly *I'll* come and work at the Bistro. You can pay *me* forty-five pounds a week!

Peter Make your mind up. A moment ago you were screaming for a divorce.

Polly I'd like to drag you by the nose through every court in England. The divorce court. The appeal court. The House of Lords. Unfortunately I'm pregnant again so I shan't have the time.

Peter What did you say?

Polly I said I'd like to drag you by the——

Peter I know what you said! You can't possibly be pregnant!

Polly (*smugly*) Well, I am. (*She sits*)

Robin Congratulations! I think this calls for champagne.

Peter That'll do. We're not launching a naval frigate! (*To Polly*) Are you sure?

Polly I'll admit that the possibility seems rather remote. But if you'll just cast your mind back to one evening when the deep-freeze broke down at the Bistro. You came home very early and rather drunk.

Peter That was eight, nine, ten weeks ago!

Polly (*smugly*) That's right.

Peter Why, in heaven's name, didn't you tell me before?

Polly I was saving it up! Until we had a row.

Robin Yes, pretty powerful ammunition that.

Emma Shut up, Robin!

Peter I just haven't got the stamina for another baby! I can't go through with it. (*To Robin*) She's insufferable when she's pregnant.

Emma It's a difficult time for a woman.

Robin It's an impossible time for a man. (*To Peter*) Does yours flop around on the sofa all day, moaning about her ankles?

Peter I only wish she did! She gallivants round the town like Superwoman. She's got this fixed idea that she mustn't give in. I'm the one that gives in. Parties every night until three in the morning. She plays tennis, she goes swimming—it's indecent!

Polly Do you want me to behave as if I was an invalid?

Peter Yes! and give me a bit of peace! And this time keep your hands off my golf clubs!

Polly Very well, dear. (*She rises*) Are you ready?

Peter (*suspicious*) Ready? Ready for what?

Polly I thought we might call in at the squash courts. We'll book for the season, you know how packed they get before breakfast. (*Going up the stairs*) Thank you for a wonderful party, Emma. I'm sure Matthew thoroughly enjoyed himself.

Peter follows Polly upstairs

Emma (*over-sweetly*) Not at all. Thank *you*. For everything you've done. (*Relenting slightly*) We'll have a natter on the phone next week.

Polly Let's all *do* something. The four of us. Go out on the town one night and live it up.

Peter The only time you can get her in a night club is when she's out here.

Polly We'll go to the Bunny Club. And then on!

Polly sails out

Peter (*looking down at Robin and Emma aghast*) You don't know what she's like when she's pregnant. Up at the crack of dawn for her exercises. Pre-natal exercises, ante-natal exercises, breathing exercises, stomach muscle exercises. Twenty-four hours a day for nine full months with her feet stuck up in the air! You walk into that house and it's like Henry Cooper's gym!

Peter exits

Robin Well well well.

Emma Is that all you can say? Well well well.

Robin It seems as good an observation as any.

Emma You come here. You infiltrate your mistress into a children's party. You behave like the complete swine that you are. And then you have the effrontery to say well well well.

Robin I wasn't saying well well well about our own particular point of no return. I was saying well well well about Peter and Polly.

Emma What about Peter and Polly.

Robin Expecting a visit from the stork.

Emma Don't be nauseating.

Robin It might be a good thing. It could pull them together.

Emma It'll tear them apart.

Robin Only if Polly lets it.

Emma What on earth has it got to do with her?

Robin She's the woman in the case. It's always the woman who lets herself go. Becomes obsessed with potty-training. Ceases to be a companion. Becomes a cabbage.

Emma I'm not a cabbage!

Robin I didn't say you, I said Polly.

Emma You said Polly and you meant me.

Robin All right, if the cap fits. If Michael Parkinson's wife can cope with babies and be on television, I don't see why other women can't.

Emma Perhaps Michael Parkinson doesn't tread birthday cake all over the floor when he's supposed to be clearing up.

Robin (*reminiscently*) You can't get BBC-two on my set.

Emma My heart bleeds for you.

Robin Your set still ticking away OK?

Emma Yes thank you.

Robin Good! Well, I'll shove off. Does that supermarket at the bottom of the hill stay open?

Emma I believe so.

Robin Good! (*He moves towards the french windows*) I'll pick up a tin of dinner on the way home. Oh for . . . ! That is all I needed! It's started to snow!

Emma follows Robin's glance to the french windows where the first flakes of snow are beginning to drift

Emma The end of a perfect day.

Robin Quite. Oh, by the way—very important. When Victoria Plum turns up would you ring me immediately?

Emma (*almost crying*) Is that *all* you care about? Our marriage is in shreds and all that occupies your mind is a couple of shilling exercise books.

Robin Emma, how can I get it into your head that Victoria Plum *is* important! Apart from a reprint of *Our Baby's Zoo Alphabet*, that manuscript represents the whole future output of Robin Partridge Ltd.

Polly puts her head round the door upstairs. She is carrying a balloon and other party favours

Polly We're off now, darling. Incidentally, the party's broken up. There's only one survivor. A little Pakistani girl sitting in a corner eating a tulip. She seems to be wearing some sort of national costume.

Emma She's waiting for the Embassy car. Tell Mavis to watch out for it.

Polly There's no sign of Mavis. Adam and Charity are amusing themselves. (*She nods towards the french windows*) They're playing at snow-storms.

Robin and Emma stare at the falling "snow"

It's little bits of paper they're throwing out of the window. I believe that's how it's done in the theatre. It's quite effective, isn't it?

A terrifying thought has crossed Robin's mind and he continues to stare hard. Emma is only tired

Emma What are they tearing up now?

Polly Oh—just some old exercise books.

Polly goes out

Emma's fears are also roused. They both watch the "snow". Robin crosses to the french window and plucks a "snowflake" as it falls. He examines it and reads

Robin "She *was* excited!" (*He holds up the snowflake*) Victoria Plum.

Emma (*nervously*) I'm terribly sorry, Robin. I can't think how they got hold of it.

Robin No. You realize that this is the end of a long, hard road, I suppose? I have spent years of my life building up a business concern which your children are at this moment throwing out of the upstairs window. (*Calling out*) Will you stop that!

Emma (*still nervously*) Surely it's not as bad as all that, Robin?

Robin The only copy of Mervyn Liversedge's latest work is being cast to the winds, and you say, surely it's not as bad as all that!

Emma You'll have to tell him that it was an accident. Take him out to a posh lunch.

Robin My dear Emma, the only information that friend Liversedge will require from me will be the quickest route to Messrs Heinemann and Co.

Emma Let him go. Mervyn Liversedge isn't the only author in the world.

Robin The royalties on the reprint of *Our Baby's Zoo Alphabet* would not keep this family in shoe repairs.

Emma It's only Adam who's heavy on shoes. Charity's quite good really.

Robin (*dropping his "snowflake"*) Well, there goes the House of Partridge. As you say—the end of a perfect day.

Emma I'm sorry, Robin.

Robin So am I. I mean—I'm sorry things didn't work out.

Emma Do you mean the reconciliation or the divorce?

Robin Either. Both. Whichever you wanted.

Emma Which did you want?

Robin I don't know. I can't afford to keep two homes going, I know that much. Perhaps I could start printing dirty books in a basement bed-sitter.

Emma You *could* have a room here if you want one.

Robin I was hoping you'd say that.

Emma Because you want to save on rent or because you want to come back?

Robin Because I want to come back.

Emma Perhaps we'd better have that dinner together after all.

Robin (*suddenly exploding*) We can't afford bloody dinner! Wheeler's? I'd be hard pressed to stand you a night out at the corner fish shop.

Emma We could stay in. I've got some steakburgers in the fridge. And there's lots of trifle to be eaten up.

Robin pulls a face

It won't be too bad, Robin.

Robin (*mistaking her meaning*) No. Perhaps the worst is behind us. It was only the kids, Emma. They're getting older now.

Emma I have a horrible feeling that the worst is still to come. They haven't had chicken-pox yet—or mumps.

Robin No, neither have I.

Emma Adam's still wetting the bed—he'll be wetting the bed when he's twenty-one. Charity's seven years old and she can't read—she'll never be able to read—and if she can't read why does she go to bed every night clutching the Bible?

Robin Perhaps she's going to be a nun.

Emma There are days when I know for a certain fact that they're both insane. The way they stand and stare at you—Adam with his tongue hanging out dribbling—Charity with her eyes crossed for hours on end. She does it on purpose, the specialist said so. And why won't Adam eat. Anything. Anything at all, except Mars bars. Did you see him at tea? He'll have false teeth by the time he's ten. Are you sure you want to come back?

Robin Yes please.

Emma Go and see what they're up to now.

Robin goes upstairs. Halfway up he pauses

Robin Steakburgers, eh? We could eat them on our laps and watch the old movie! In colour!

Emma Just a minute, Robin! Can I get one thing quite clear. Are you saying that you want to come back to me so that you can watch BBC-two?

Robin (*after a moment's thought*) I'll go and see what the kids are doing.

Robin goes out

Emma shakes her head, and tries to re-arrange some of the pieces of torn-up exercise book into their correct sequence. She forms a word and sweeps the pieces on to the floor in disgust

Emma Basil Banana!

Robin appears upstairs

Robin I say! Come up here, quick!
Emma What are they doing now?
Robin No, it's not the kids—it's Mavis!
Emma What's Mavis doing?
Robin She's having a bath!

Emma stares at him and then breaks into hysterical laughter. Robin too starts laughing as—

the CURTAIN *falls*

FURNITURE AND PROPERTY LIST

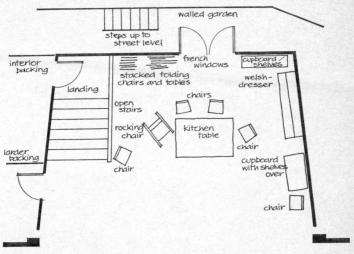

ACT I

SCENE 1

On stage: Kitchen table. *On it:* cloth, box of balloons, box of Kleenex, bunch of party "favours", various dishes, cutlery, party decorations, bowl of whipped cream and whisk

Welsh dresser. *On it:* trays with plates of sausage rolls, jellies, biscuits, cakes, etc., party decorations, assorted oddments, birthday cake with 5 candles, box of matches. *On shelves:* cups, saucers, plates. *In drawers:* string, meat skewer, thimble, pair of pliers, dish-cloth, cutlery, table cloths, general dressing

Cupboard. *On top:* bottle of cooking sherry, glasses, plates of sand-wiches, etc. *In it:* hammer, hacksaw, dressing. *On shelves above:* glasses, general kitchen utensils and dressing. *On floor below:* "Gonk"

Rocking chair

5 kitchen chairs

2 card tables, stacked against wall

4 folding chairs, stacked against wall

On walls: child's paintings

Window curtains

Off stage: 2 children's coats **(Emma)**
              2 folding card tables **(Peter)**
              Letters, birthday cards, bill, in envelopes, and large manilla envelope
                   containing manuscript **(Peter)**
              Live white rabbit **(Tom)**
              Suitcase labelled Mr Lollipop and plywood conjuring apparatus
                 (Tom)
              Trick flower bouquet **(Tom)**
              Book **(Emma)**
              Trick string of flags **(Tom)**
              Broken pottery figure **(Mavis)**
              Pedal car **(Tom)**
              Child's goose costume **(Polly)**
              Bent car number plate **(Robin)**
              2 broken roses **(Robin)**
              Wand **(Tom)**
              Pedal car, identical with Tom's **(Robin)**
              Table-knife with pat of butter **(Mavis)**
              Pats of butter in dish **(Mavis)**
              Sawn-off pedal car **(Peter)**
              2 glove puppets, one of "Sooty" **(Tom)**
              Miniature bow tie **(Mavis)**
Personal: **Tom:** business card

ACT II

SCENE 1

Off stage: Several party hats **(Mavis)**
              Pirate party hat **(Tom)**
              Magic card castle **(Tom)**   ⎱
              "Mr Lollipop" card **(Tom)** ⎰ in tail-coat
Personal: **Tom:** writ, business card
            Robin: diary, pen

SCENE 2

Set: Room in chaos: chairs overturned, remnants of food on table and
              floor, cloths awry and stained, burst balloons, torn paper hats, etc.
Off stage: Balloon, party favours **(Polly)**
              Torn-up exercise book pages **(Stage Management)**
Personal: **Tom:** writ
            Robin: propelling pencil

EFFECTS PLOT

ACT I

Cue 1   As CURTAIN rises   (Page 1)
           Sounds of children's party and music; general party noises
           from the off-stage living-room. These sounds swell out
           through the Act whenever the landing door is opened

ACT II

SCENE 1

Cue 2   As CURTAIN rises   (Page 32)
           Party noises whenever landing door is opened. Continue
           until Cue 3

Cue 3   **Emma:** ". . . every time you open this door!"   (Page 38)
           Emma opens landing door
           Total silence from living-room

Cue 4   **Tom:** ". . . into something decent!"   (Page 41)
           Mavis enters
           Sounds of children

Cue 5   During scene drop   (Page 42)
           Loud party noises, children running downstairs, eating
           food, running up again

SCENE 2

Cue 6   As CURTAIN rises   (Page 42)
           Children's voices very loud

Cue 7   **Mavis:** "SHURRUP!"   (Page 42)
           Instant silence

Cue 8   **Sophie:** ". . . has she had a bath yet?"   (Page 43)
           Front doorbell rings

LIGHTING PLOT

Property fittings required: pendant (dressing only)
Interior. A kitchen. The same scene throughout

ACT I   Afternoon
To open: General effect of late autumn afternoon light
No cues

ACT II, SCENE 1.   Afternoon
To open: As previous Act
No cues

ACT II, SCENE 2.   Afternoon
To open: As previous Act
No cues

MADE AND PRINTED IN GREAT BRITAIN BY
LATIMER TREND & COMPANY LTD PLYMOUTH